TO THE END

TO THE END

Queer Writers on Divorce and Liberation

EDITED BY Morty Diamond, LCSW

North Atlantic Books
Huichin, unceded Ohlone land
Berkeley, California

North Atlantic Books
Huichin, unceded Ohlone land
2526 Martin Luther King Jr. Way
Berkeley, CA 94704 USA
www.northatlanticbooks.com

Cover design by Jess Morphew
Book design by Happenstance Type-O-Rama

Acquisitions editor and production editor: Gillian Hamel
Copyeditor: Brent Winter • Proofreader: Melanie Demmer

North Atlantic Books's publications are distributed to the US trade and internationally by Penguin Random House Publisher Services. For further information, visit our website at www.northatlanticbooks.com.

The authorized representative in the EU for product safety and compliance is Eucomply OÜ, Pärnu mnt 139b-14, 11317 Tallinn, Estonia, hello@eucompliancepartner.com, +33757690241.

Library of Congress Cataloging-in-Publication Data

Names: Diamond, Morty, 1975– editor
Title: To the end : LGBTQ+ writers on love, loss, and liberation in divorce / edited by Morty Diamond, LCSW.
Description: Berkeley, California : North Atlantic Books, [2026] | Summary: "24 stories of queer divorce—a groundbreaking book of essays that unflinchingly explores love, loss, and liberation beyond the confines of cishet marriage"—Provided by publisher.
Identifiers: LCCN 2026007555 (print) | LCCN 2026007556 (ebook) | ISBN 9798889843986 paperback | ISBN 9798889843993 epub
Subjects: LCSH: Same-sex divorce | Sexual minorities—Family relationships | Interpersonal conflict
Classification: LCC HQ825 .T62 2026 (print) | LCC HQ825 (ebook)
LC record available at https://lccn.loc.gov/2026007555
LC ebook record available at https://lccn.loc.gov/2026007556

1 2 3 4 5 6 7 8 9 KPC 31 30 29 28 27 26

Printed in the United States of America

Contents

Introduction

MORTY DIAMOND

I have become known as the "Prince of Queer Divorce" among my friend group. If you see me at a pool party or potluck, I'm the one asking queer, trans, and nonbinary community members, "Are you divorced?"

The shifting balance from "married" to "divorced" is an all-consuming experience. When I began navigating my divorce, the connection to married life dissolved, and I discovered a keen interest in the phenomenology of how other queer and trans people experience divorce. I became an utter nerd for queer divorce and fell headlong into engaging discussions from chat rooms to bar stools. I have entered Zoom rooms, made phone calls, and text chatted with other newly divorced queers to compile and learn hard-won insights that would help me frame my own experience. I read every written word I could find on queer divorce, and I devoured all that was available to me in my quest to know the subject matter intimately.

This book emerged from my unwavering attention to the subject of LGBTQ+ divorce and my fervent belief that it is imperative we talk about this underdiscussed subject. I am grateful to each writer in this book, as they have built a beautiful mosaic on the magical, provocative, painful, and compelling experience of LGBTQ+ divorce.

I dove into media, history books, and Youtube videos to find out who the heck we were—queer, trans, and nonbinary people who had agreed to frame their life around legal marriage only to then be cast out of that picture, either by force or willingly. It's quite strenuous to write about divorce and extract the wisdom of having been married. Divorce is a full Venn diagram of every possible battle one could consider: legal, emotional, financial, physical, spiritual, and familial. It is difficult to take stock of what your life amounts to as you're busy interviewing attorneys, preparing for court showdowns, looking for a new place to call home, and establishing yourself as a newly single person. Divorce, even in its most appealing light, is often heartbreaking and alarming. Divorce is also a journey with a multitude of paths toward self-discovery. This book examines the conditions under which a marriage dissolves and how LGBTQ+ people traverse the complicated matrix of challenges within the process of divorce.

So how did we end up here? To facilitate dialogue on divorce, I had to become comfortable with hearing mine and break the silence that had permeated my marriage. I had to work with, through, and against the limits of my own divorce story.

I had already been married for eight years when *Obergefell v. Hodges* made same-sex marriage legal across the US in 2015. What mattered most on the day I walked up to the county clerk was the "M" on my driver's license (and my partner's "F") so we could be granted a marriage license. Legal documentation accurately reflecting my gender carries great significance. I came out as trans during the late '90s and endured many instances of harassment before I was able to change my driver's license to reflect my male gender identity. Right before we reached the clerk's window, I turned to my soon-to-be legal spouse and said, "I hope they're not good at clocking trans people," certain that at any given moment I'd be found out and sent away in handcuffs. Standing at the clerk's counter, we raised our hands and swore we were who we said we were and that we wanted to be married. I recall walking away from that window thinking, *Dang, that was easy.*

In 2015, many queer couples lined up to experience legal marriage for the first time. On the evening of the *Obergefell v. Hodges* ruling, the White House was lit up in a rainbow, denoting the LGBTQ+ Pride flag. I noted the level of celebration reverberating across Los Angeles, the city I had called home for most of my life. I was excited, too. The local gay bars were erupting in a parade of celebrations. Queers with wide smiles, arms outstretched to each other, jubilantly cheered with celebratory drinks held up high. I watched YouTube videos of gay men and women with ecstatic smiles on their faces, kissing on the courthouse steps. *Wow, this is so cool*, I thought. *We won this thing*. This mighty institution of marriage was ours for the taking, and many of us did.

I did not understand and would not allow myself to comprehend my faulty thinking on marriage. I seemed to be dissolving into an identity that, as it turned out, was ill-fitting. My marriage was inspired by a desire to feel protected. I received protection in the form of health benefits (which I desperately needed) and as a way to protect myself from my own transphobia. When I came out as trans at twenty-three years old, my family of origin rejected me. Though I felt held by community and friends, whose stories often reflected my own familial struggles, I had a deep well of loneliness and self-hatred brewing inside. My partner also offered me immunity from the pain of self-discovery. I was now a husband. This label wound a tight blanket around my heart, covering me with the thinnest fabric of protection against my inner struggles with my mental health and my deeply entrenched feelings of rejection and inadequacy.

I had been married for ten and a half years and had a three-and-a-half-year-old child (whom I'll call A) when I separated from my partner in November of 2019. By February 2020 my ex had decided to move from our home in Oakland, California, to her parents' house in Los Angeles. I was also planning my own move to Los Angeles, so I allowed her to take our child to her parents' home. She told me I would be able to see my child, A, soon. But this would not be the case. I sent dozens of messages to my ex, begging to set a time when I could see A. I was dumbfounded when I realized that two months had elapsed, and the word "soon" evaporated before my eyes. I hired an attorney who negotiated a temporary agreement with my ex's attorney to give me access to A. The agreement stated I was only allowed to see A during daytime hours. "Daytime hours only? Why?" I pleaded with my attorney. She said, "Your ex is playing hardball, and I want you to connect to your child immediately. It's not right, but you'll be able to see A soon. It's the best I could do."

This was the beginning of a long, unforgiving road where divorce amounted to reading horrible things my ex had written about me in court-filed paperwork, and trying to retain a sense of control as I feared my parental and personal rights were under attack. In one court document my ex wrote in a statement to the judge that I had not legally adopted our child. My ex was formulating an argument and fired a warning shot that said: *I am going after your legal rights to A.*

I never sought legal adoption because I was on the birth certificate as A's father. I never expected to need to prove my parentage. The creeping nausea of finding out how naive I was regarding the systems at play kept me awake most nights. It was humiliating and soul crushing to know that my ex—who had claimed to love me as a trans person who could not physically carry a child, nor offer my own gametes to have a baby—was now using my lived experience to harm me. The old, poisoned waters of my own internal transphobia began to run through me once again. Thoughts I hadn't encountered in years related to the stigma of being a trans person and daring to want to be a parent began to ricochet through me.

In one of the emails my attorney sent, she said: "Clearly there is no legal question that Morty is A's dad, so I am not sure why [my ex] added that he 'never took any action to adopt A or to become her legal parent' except to be needlessly cruel."

Needlessly cruel. Those words would ricochet in my body for months.

During this process I required extra support. I texted friends, called family members, sent screenshots of paperwork, and asked loved ones to remind me that I wasn't deserving of this response from my ex. When I felt I had exhausted my support system I quickly realized my need to speak directly, face to face, with other queer divorcees. In February 2023 I launched the To the End Salon, an online group where LGBTQ+ divorcees come together to discuss anything and everything about divorce. The salon continues to this day.

My body was also taking a big hit. The seemingly endless pain I was experiencing would be mitigated with healing massages by a trusted community member. It wouldn't take more than a few minutes, as her hands released tension from my shoulders, before tears would roll down my cheeks. "You don't deserve this," she would whisper. "Try to let it go."

Throughout the divorce I experienced my ex as cagey and deceitful. I began to realize I was divorcing someone I didn't know. Had she become someone I couldn't trust to be thoughtful or caring, or was this the person I had been married to all along? Finally, the court date came. We managed to formulate most of our agreement without the court's assistance, but my ex was asking the court for full legal custody of A. As we sat in the hallway waiting to be called into court, my ex's attorney called my attorney over. My attorney had a grim look on her face as she walked back to me and said, "She's not going to pursue full legal custody." I had spent thousands of dollars and countless hours prepping the argument for shared legal custody; and in one blink it was over. My attorney said, "A lot of hindsight occurs on the courthouse steps."

Finally, my legal divorce was complete. Unfortunately, my fight to remain seen as my child's parent continued. One summer day in 2023, when A was seven years old, she was in my living room talking to her mother on speakerphone when I heard my ex say, "Did Mr. Diamond make sure to . . ." and every cell in my body erupted with rage and sadness in equal measure. When A got off the phone, she looked at me with a confused, worried expression and said, "Why is Mommy calling you Mr. Diamond?"

I simply said, "Honey, I don't know, but it's not right. I'm your Dad."

Two years ago, I walked into my child's classroom and saw over her desk the "family poster" she had made with my ex. On it was a photo of the sperm donor and his mother. I searched for my face. It was not there. This week, the last week of September 2025, the sperm donor's mother passed away. In her obituary it names my child as her "grandchild."

For years, I have thought about family court intervention. I believe my ex was engaging in parental alienation, and the sperm donor was going against the legal document he signed to not be seen as part of our family. I wanted to make it "right," to make my ex and the sperm donor culpable for their wrongdoings. I engaged an attorney who said, "To be forthright, this kind of alienation is not something the court cares about." The attorney also encouraged me to be careful, as discrimination against transgender parents is endemic in the family court system.

This book began with a list of questions I had churning in my head:

- Is the married queer couple the ultimate ideal and a demonstration of our long-held desire to be seen as just like hetero couples?
- For queer people: Is your lens on marriage equality smudged or broken after divorce?
- Are the battles faced in family court different for queer and trans people?
- Some of us looked to marriage as a way to legitimize or normalize our lives. Did divorce change this?
- What lessons about LGBTQ+ identity do we discover through divorce?

As I began to write the call for submissions for the book, I felt a jolt of fear. Did anyone actually care about queer divorce stories? The major publications of legacy media have never taken a close look at queer divorce stories. I was hard pressed to find any magazine or newspaper articles unpacking the fundamental changes LGBTQ+ divorcees are experiencing in light of the legalities affecting our lives. Fiction and nonfiction books from the last five years focusing on queer divorce narratives would fill a small area of your bookshelf. These books are largely written by cis queer or bisexual women, though not all. Titles I read in preparation for this book include *The Rules Do Not Apply* by Ariel Levy, *In the Dream House* by Carmen Maria Machado, and *How to Burn a Rainbow* by Karl Dunn. As a widely read fiction book with a queer divorce storyline, Miranda July's *All Fours* came to embody what I believe to be the literary zeitgeist of dissolving satisfaction with marriage for LGBTQ+ people. I found queer divorce stories hidden in the not-so-hidden world of social media. Facebook groups, Reddit rooms, Substack pages, and Discord channels were teeming with descriptions of queer divorce in real time: the phases of divorce, changing desires, managing shock and grief. All of it.

I scoured the internet looking for queer divorcees willing to write their story for a larger audience. I emailed friends and colleagues asking to be connected to writers who were freely talking about their divorce. I sent the call for submissions to every queer literary website I could find. I searched the web for therapists who publicly said they worked with queer divorcees, and I emailed them a request to share the book information with their clients.

Queer, trans, and nonbinary writers would eventually email me proclaiming they were excited to find out about the book and then apologizing for not being able to tell their story. Too messy, too scary, too worried about retribution, too much drama already . . . I heard it all. Still, there was agreement that someone needed to bring the microphone to the wonderfully diverse group of queer divorcees and crack into the depths of insight, feeling, and history present in this underrepresented slice of queer life.

Many writers assailed this book as problematic and said queers did not want to discuss getting divorced because it gives fodder to the far-right agenda to destroy our right to be legally married. Although I do agree that our stories are often used as ammunition against us, I do not believe we should refrain from discussing our stories in public. For me, to shut down conversations on queer lives and exclude ourselves from freely recording our stories imposes more negative consequences than allowing them to exist.

Gradually, stories began to trickle in. After a deep Google session looking for "trans divorce stories," I discovered that Thomas Beattie had gone through a challenging and harrowing divorce, so I emailed him. Shanna Katz mentioned their divorce on social media, which prompted me to send them a message about this book. I sent email requests to Jacoby Ballard, Chris E. Vargas, and Syd Yang, all of whom I know through personal or professional community connections. I have been a fan of Sassafras Patterdale's work for close to a decade, and after reading their recently published article on divorce (one of the very few queer divorce essays I found on a major publication website), I requested a longer-form personal essay for this book. I sent the call for submissions to therapists, writers, and anyone who told me they knew a queer divorcee. All told, this book took three years to come to fruition.

Before we can discuss how divorce impacts queer lives, we need to know a bit about legal LGBTQ+ marriage. The Williams Institute, situated in the UCLA School of Law, estimates that roughly 57 percent of "same sex couples"[1] have married since *Obergefell* became law. It is neat and tidy to explore data on "same-sex marriage." However, this data eschews the multitudes of other marriages that might fit within the LGBTQ+ experience. For example, we do not have concrete data on legal marriage occurring between nonbinary partners, bisexual partners of different genders, hetero-focused marriages where one person is queer or trans, and so on. The largest transgender survey in the US did not question respondents about marital status.[2] A small-sample-size survey from KFF and *The Washington Post* posited that trans people in the US are "half as likely to be currently married than non-trans adults."[3]

I often hear about a monolithic "we" who pushed the buttons and lifted the levers to hoist same-sex marriage all the way up the legal ladder and stamp it at the most important human rights issue of this century for LGBTQ+ communities. The truth is, the years of legal setbacks, political actions, and attorney bills necessary to bring same-sex marriage to the US Supreme Court could only be funded by the very wealthy among us. Same-sex marriage needed individuals like Evan Wolfson, a gay man who, as an attorney, understood both the complex underpinnings of making a legal case for same-sex marriage and the funding needed to make it a plausible fight to win in court.

We cannot forget there is also a "we" who stood up and exclaimed how awful it is to be absorbed into fighting for the right to be married, thus bringing us closer to the people who want nothing more than to see queer lives and culture dismantled.

For most of my life I have shared space with queer community members who have a deep disdain for legal same-sex marriage. Queer elders who formed local activist circles back in the early 2000s in the San Francisco Bay Area warned me that same-sex marriage would be a backslide into the hegemonic forces that many queers were so desperate to rid ourselves of. I was told the fracturing of the queer community in terms of power and privilege is precisely why we have legal same-sex marriage. Same-sex marriage had a seamless argument ("equality") and became an easy news story ("we just want to get married"). Meanwhile, the day-to-day challenges of queer life, housing, medication access, HIV rates, and underemployment went neglected and were ultimately fought for only within grassroots initiatives. I don't need to hypothesize as to why these issues were not at the forefront of the queer movement. The fragmentation across race and class in the early history of the LGBTQ+ civil rights movement was profound. Mainstream gay culture routinely ignored trans activists, including Sylvia Rivera and Marsha P. Johnson, and dismissed the possibility that they could be an integral part of the queer civil rights movement.

I want to be clear: This book is not an antimarriage treatise. The essays in this book explore how legal marriage can (and should) be seen as both an asset to queer life and a problematic institution. In the US, it is fairly rare for an institution to regard marginalized individuals and families as its main benefactors. Many of us do not get to the place of critical conversations regarding the legal systems that interpret and enforce laws without these systems first failing us. This book illuminates and analyzes the institution of marriage through the lens of first-person experience. I believe this book enables engagement and opens up conversations to discover what divorce reveals about contemporary queer relations.

Stating that liberation or a liberatory way of living is not based on marriage dismisses the different paths of queer and trans people. I look to examples like Precious Brady Davis and her husband, Myles, Black trans activists who are married and raising children together.[4] Prentiss Hemphill, a well-known Black queer activist, says their marriage is one of growth and value.[5] Writer Roxane Gay says her marriage to wife Debbie Millman has been "a joyful adventure."[6]

I hope LGBTQ+ individuals use this book as a guide to help them interrogate whether or not legal marriage is right for them. If you are an LGBTQ+ married person, I would like for this book to guide your discovery about what is at stake in the event that your marriage ends in divorce. I have found that many queer, trans, and nonbinary people become critical of the institution of marriage after divorce. I also see people breaking the colonialist structures of gender, romance, and relationships after divorce. This book is meant to grease the wheels for conversations—with yourself and with your community—on what is possible after divorce. I would like for this book to germinate ideas about what community-based support might look like for queer divorced couples. And lastly, I hope this book encourages integral conversations on how we heal ourselves after relational endings.

My desire to seek the meaning of divorce for all LGBTQ+ people through personal narrative is partly based on feeling invalidated by and erased from the larger structures of power and privilege we are currently grappling with. Queers in general, and certainly those who live beyond the binary, continue to experience an epistemic injustice looming over our lives. We are also in a crisis of holding onto historical information regarding queer and trans lives; thus, we must mobilize our own stories to carry the torch for examining the process of our lives.

What's so different about divorce for LGBTQ+ people? Well, quite a lot. I'd like to break down a few important facts and social/emotional issues that are specific to LGBTQ+ couples as they navigate legal divorce.

First, it's essential we focus on the fact that LGBTQ+ married couples in the US are in extreme fear that *Obergefell* will be overturned and the Supreme Court will dismantle its existence. Just this is enough to draw a pretty strong line in the sand stating that, yes, queer people are experiencing marriage differently from heterosexual people.

A legal divorce can propel LGBTQ+ people into deeper institutional harm. Queer people often become lulled into believing that the court, its laws, and its attorneys can protect them from the harms the system itself is perpetrating. Even without the use of an attorney or mediator, the divorce process must include a judge's approval. In the US, each state governs its own family court system, which, in a divorce proceeding, regulates things such as property division, child custody, and residency requirements, to name just a few. From state to state, these processes vary to such a wild degree that there would be no way to encapsulate the various outcomes LGBTQ+ experience; the outcomes are often inconsistent from case to case. To terminate a marriage is to get slapped in the face with rules, regulations, laws, legal jargon, and complex procedures. Depending on the state or even the county you are divorcing in, your chances of getting a judge who has familiarity with LGBTQ+ lives might be nil. I have heard of and read about far too many cases of judicial bias where queer people are presumed to be lacking as parents or are denied parenthood altogether.[7] Only a few of these cases make it to the news cycle. We have no real way to examine how often antigay bias occurs within the family court systems. What we do know is this is not a bygone concern for LGBTQ+ people. These cases are often hidden from sight due to shame and stigma.

Divorce is a financial nightmare, and this is a particularly salient issue with regard to LGBTQ+ lives. Economic and financial surveys report that LGBTQ+ individuals have lower annual household incomes than cishet adults nationwide.[8] Another study found that 47 percent of LGBTQ+ people of color live in a low-income household.[9] LGBTQ+ people consistently face higher unemployment rates and high rates of workplace discrimination, both of which affect overall financial stability.

The family court system is extremely difficult to navigate without legal representation. In California, family law attorneys charge an average of $300 to $500 an hour. Many LGBTQ+ people who lack the means to retain or consult an attorney feel an increased vulnerability in the family court system, not only with regard to parental rights but also potential loss of financial assets. In the US, each state takes a different approach toward dividing marital assets in the divorce process. Without an attorney, it is difficult to learn what an equitable distribution of assets looks like. I have heard plenty of queer divorce stories in which the one who had more financial stability hired an attorney to exploit loopholes, hide assets, and protect parental rights, while the one without an attorney became overwhelmed and was not able to ensure a fair settlement.

Currently, trans people in the US are being stripped of their freedoms, one by one. The family court system is no less a culprit in the fracturing of trans rights. In modern-day America, judges infuse the court system with their ideologies to engage in state-sanctioned violence against trans and queer people. Depending on your geographic location, you may find a family court judge very willing to strip a trans parent of their legal rights to their children. Judges in red states don't need to be convinced that trans people are unfit parents. Statistics on this topic are difficult to estimate, because we don't see many trans people willing to engage in a public outcry against the child welfare or family court system. Trans people have already been seen as dangerous to the cisnormative family structure, and they face special risks when entering an institution filled with individuals who seek to dehumanize their experience.

Legal and economic advantages fall away during the divorce process. We lose health care, access to housing, and other necessities of life. These are the same vulnerabilities that many heterosexual couples would face; however, the consequences are more pronounced for LBGTQ+ people, as we are a vulnerable population, which makes these losses much greater. The fact that 28 percent of LGBTQ+ youth have been homeless at one point in their lives gets to the heart of the queer adult experience of losing one's home once again.[10]

One of the most essential components of this book is the vast amount of emotion expressed in each essay. There is not one essay that does not go bone deep toward the failings and discoveries of divorce. I wanted to include a wide variety of the emotional and relational aspects of ending relationships in this book.

Chris Vargas does an amazing job of describing how the end of a domestic partnership can still feel like a divorce. W. E. Cuthbert details a surviving relationship with his former spouse post-transition and postdivorce. Child custody and coparenting stories demonstrate some of the most concerning areas of divorce. One of my goals was to find as many permutations of what a post-divorce queer life looks like with children in the mix. Tahnie Holcomb's piece explores the delicate balance of sharing custody after leaving a marriage mired in domestic violence. Jacoby Ballard sends the reader on an exploration of the logistical, spiritual, and social aspects of holding space for his child postdivorce.

I am a big believer in defusing mental health stigmas through narrative work. Many essays in this book speak to the emotional and psychological impact of divorce and the ways in which a divorce often requires a recovery process.

Queer divorcees often discuss their anxiety over the unclear terrain of divorce proceedings. Many queer divorcees also recognize how their marriage engendered feelings of adequacy and safety that might feel especially stabilizing if living in an unwelcoming part of the world. Postdivorce feelings often turn toward shame, stigma, and fear. The essay by Jálynn T. Castleman is foundational reading for learning how the process of a tumultuous divorce creates internal turmoil and tension that require immense strength to endure.

The essays from Paisley Cornell, Kira Ry, R. M. H., and Nailah Rose explore the salient but less-discussed topic of divorce as an act of coming into alignment with your sense of self and your needs. Often this is a coming-out narrative wherein the divorce stems from one person no longer being able to stay within the structure of a heterosexual relationship. There is a lot of charged energy in these stories, as the predominant media spectacle is one in which queer and trans people who leave heteronormative relationships are often vilified and attacked.

I found almost no material or media on the Black queer experience of divorce, and I felt this book would not be complete without these stories. I am thankful to have essays from Jálynn T. Castleman, Nailah Rose, Janice Vogel, and Teré Fowler-Chapman, each one highlighting different arenas of subjectivity and lived experience of divorce.

I am very interested in how sex and sexuality weave in and out of divorce. In Sassafras Patterdale's piece, the rarely discussed relationship dynamic of a 24/7 Daddy/boi power exchange unravels in the midst of legal divorce. I was floored while reading Marina Montes de Oca's piece on finding liberation in reopening the chapter of first dates and reignited pleasure in exploring sex after divorce. Liz Hardwick's essay reels with the tension between the end of the family constellation and metabolizing the raw arena of touch from new lovers.

For many writers, marriage signaled a measure of conventional success that allowed them to rise above the underlying currents of stigma and shame.

In my ongoing discussions with other queer divorcees I discovered that shame, stigma, and a feeling of failure may come from beyond the family of origin, beyond the inner working of our sadness, to include queer community, as much as I'd like to believe the opposite. The essays from Shào Fù and Dominika Bednarska explore the terrain of sadness, shame, and rejection from within queer divorce. Dominika's piece is also a powerful commentary on the end of married life when losing a wife and a caregiver.

I also looked for essays that explored and interrogated the models of success and failure in the binary model of married/unmarried. Shanna Katz Kattari and Leonardo Kattari have a piece that may be the first published divorce essay written by both divorcees. I love this essay for its nod to queerly "uncoupling" and finding a path past divorce where two people can remain a dedicated queer family to each other.

The stories in this book are meant to help individuals and communities affected by LGBTQ+ divorce find guidance that is rooted in both lived experience and practical insight. I believe that moving forward, the ways in which divorce impacts queer identities will shape queer culture. The unique circumstances of queer divorce are such that we are on the precipice of an evolution of understanding of what marriage offers us. I believe this book may encourage a new definition of failure and/or success in relationships, and open up a conversation on the necessity of the marriage/divorce arc for the queer community.

Notes

1 UCLA School of Law Williams Institute. n.d. "Same Sex Couples." https://williamsinstitute.law.ucla.edu/subpopulations/same-sex-couples/ (accessed February 19, 2026).

2 U.S. Trans Survey. 2022. "Health and Wellbeing: Findings from the 2022 US Trans Survey." https://ustranssurvey.org/.

3 Lindsey Dawson, Jennifer Kates, Grace Sparks, and Ashley Kirzinger. 2023. "Trans People in the U.S.: Identities, Demographics, and Wellbeing." KFF, September 28. www.kff.org/other-health/trans-people-in-the-u-s-identities-demographics-and-wellbeing/#:~:text=Marital%20Status.,been%20married%20(25%25%20vs.

4 Jake Wittich. 2023. "This Black, Trans Chicago Couple Is Breaking Barriers and Inspiring Younger Queer People with Their Love." *Block Club Chicago*, June 29. https://blockclubchicago.org/2023/06/29/this-black-trans-chicago-couple-is-breaking-barriers-and-inspiring-younger-queer-people-with-their-love/.

5 Jonathan Fields, host. 2024. *Good Life Project*. "How to Change Ourselves and Our World: Prentiss Hemphill." Acast Network August 26th, Podcast, 1:00:02. https://www.goodlifeproject.com/podcast/embodiment-for-healing-and-social-change-with-prentis-hemphill/.

6 Roxane Gay (@roxanegay74). 2024. "Six years ago, Debbie and I went on our first date. I didn't Google her or know anything about her. She asked me out on a 'proper date' which was endlessly charming." Instagram, October 29. https://www.instagram.com/p/DA64mLYtSRX/?hl=en.

7 Amy Maitner. 2019. "Judicial Bias Against LGBT Parents in Custody Disputes." *University of Florida Journal of Law and Public Policy*, 30(1). https://scholarship.law.ufl.edu/jlpp/vol30/iss1/5.

8 Center for LGBTQ Economic Advancement and Research. n.d. "The LGBTQI+ Economic and Financial Survey." https://lgbtq-economics.org/research/leaf-report-2023/#:~:text=LGBTQI+%20people%20reported%20losing%20the,%25%20of%20non%2DLGBTQI+%20respondents (accessed February 19, 2025).

9 UCLA School of Law Williams Institute. 2022. "Nearly Half of LGBT People of Color Live in Low-Income Households." January 27. https://williamsinstitute.law.ucla.edu/press/race-comparison-press-release/.

10 Trevor Project. 2022. "Homelessness and Housing Instability Among LGBTQ Youth." February 3. https://www.thetrevorproject.org/research-briefs/homelessness-and-housing-instability-among-lgbtq-youth-feb-2022/.

An Elephant's Tale

SYD YANG

"It's the choice we're fighting for," J and I would argue with friends, as the marriage equality debates began to build national momentum. We were living together in Oakland when San Francisco Mayor Gavin Newsom declared marriage legal to all couples, regardless of gender, in the city of San Francisco.

It was exhilarating, those early days, witnessing a deluge of tears and joy as queer, gay, lesbian, and trans couples lined up outside city hall to make a choice that had legally been withheld for so long. The collective energy in the Bay Area was sparkling and bright. We celebrated and we made critiques. We waded through undercurrents of urgency as folks rushed to get married for fear that the right to do so might get taken away. I quickly learned that marriage was an assumed destination in many of the lesbian circles I found myself in professionally at the time. The question, it seemed, was less about whether we wanted to get married than about when we would do it. The pressure to participate came on strong:

"You've been together for years and are living together. When are you going to City Hall?"

"You're already domestic partners, right? Just get married!"

"But you can get married now! When are you going to City Hall?"

The thing is, I didn't want to get married. I had never wanted to be married. I believed marriage was a patriarchal, colonial form of ownership that made my skin crawl. Somehow, though, having the option of legal marriage tugged J and me into different conversations about our relationship from those we'd been having until then.

I knew I wanted to be with J, but I didn't think marriage was the answer to a future together. There were many ways to protect our rights. A few months earlier, we had attended a "How to Protect Yourself Legally" workshop for queer couples that was hosted by the National Center for Lesbian Rights. Sure, there were significantly more documents to sign if you didn't want to get married, but circumventing "marriage" seemed possible. I liked this route much better than getting married.

Even so, I was adamantly for marriage equality, although it wasn't so I could get legally married. It wasn't because I thought marriage was an answer to homophobia and oppression. It wasn't because I believe that love wins or that love is love. (Hot take: It doesn't and it's not, but that's a conversation for a different time.) It was because I believed everyone deserves the right to choose . . . and for a whirlwind month in early 2004, J and I embraced the possibility to choose.

We chose each other. We chose a committed future together, for the long term, and we chose to not get married.

A year later, when we split up, the only word I could find to describe my experience of our breakup was *divorce*. Even so, it always came with a caveat: "No, no, we didn't get married back then," I would say, shrugging. "But, you know, we're queer. We get to queer what marriage is, so now we get to also queer divorce."

Fourteen years later, I found myself signing legal divorce papers for the state of California, rendering an end to a relationship where we had made a different choice. Choosing to get legally married had, at the time, seemed like a practical decision to improve my access to health care on my terms. Choosing to end the relationship, however, became an annoyingly bureaucratic endeavor that felt like being punished. Though this was technically a divorce, that word never rolled easily off my tongue in this situation. Legally, it felt as if I was acknowledging participation in a heteronormative ritual, one I was embarrassed to admit I had wanted. This divorce did not feel nearly as queer as that first big breakup with J.

I do use the term *divorce* now, mostly as a lazy shorthand to refer to that last complicated breakup when speaking with straight folks. It's just easier, I find. Fewer questions to answer, fewer feelings to engage.

Avoiding feelings is what I'm good at.

Well, that's not entirely true. My double-Scorpio self is side-eyeing me as I write that. I do love feelings. I get off on diving deep into the morass of emotional secrets and intrigue. I did not, however, want to marinate in any of the feelings stirred up by that second "divorce." They were just too complicated, I told myself: *Head down, Syd. Just keep moving forward.*

For five years, my inner voice echoed a popular refrain: "Just keep swimming, just keep swimming," on repeat. "Don't look back."

I sank my body into the proverbial couch at my therapist's office twice a week. I sat myself down on my meditation cushion several times a day, staying long past the timers I would set. I stopped writing and got back into running. I avoided dating, my body refusing to engage with the wounds it knew were still bleeding out, wounds that tugged at decades of body shame, wounds that defiantly refused to heal when treated with neglect. Less than a year after the second breakup, COVID showed up, and suddenly, focusing all my energy on caring for others felt much more appealing than tending to my own wounds.

That is not to say I wasn't healing. I was. I was looking at my own harmful patterns, burrowing deeper into my recovery, getting intimate with attachment styles and wounds, understanding covert narcissistic abuse, and eventually I found myself building up the courage to confront my complex PTSD from childhood emotional and religious abuse. And yet, there was still something I was actively avoiding, something that was keeping me cut off from what I longed for the most—intimate connection and being loved. The elephant in the room that everyone else could see, but not me:

"Your walls are hurting people, Syd."

Oh, that elephant.

Here's the thing. I really like elephants. I marvel at how they move slowly and seem to find ritual in beginnings and endings. They are profoundly wise. I fell in love with elephants in 2005, when J and I spent a day caring for them at a sanctuary in northern Thailand. Elephants are divinely magical beings. If there is an elephant in the room with me, I will fight to keep that elephant around, it appears. As this one shape-shifted into a reinforced fortress around me, I felt safe. Perhaps even safe enough to come undone.

I didn't want anyone else to see how I had failed—because divorce is a failure, right? That's what I kept telling myself. For years I had insisted that marriage was the right choice for me, that this marriage was the life I had always wanted, even as doubt followed me around every day. I clung tight to the illusion of marriage as an achievement of relational ease; a public affirmation of being loved. Somewhere in the cellular structure of my being, I had subscribed to a myth of marriage that I had been fed growing up: Marriage is the ideal relationship form. Fight for it. Contort yourself to fit in it. This is how you will be happy.

An impressive thing about building walls is that not only do they block others from getting in; they are also able to block the builder from seeing what they are hiding. Elephants are infinitely cuter than shame. I didn't want to look critically at which beliefs had gotten me here, to this place of an unraveling marriage. I wanted to point fingers and be perceived as strong. I wanted to be angry while pretending I was bigger than my anger. Above all, I didn't want to hurt anymore.

What I was unwilling to admit, even to myself, was that getting married was about surrendering to a mythology of love that told me I would be saved, that marriage was the answer to brokenheartedness, and that once married, everyone would know I was good enough to be loved. A part of me had fallen for the fairytale that my prince would find me and save me from the big bad wolves (my childhood trauma), who had convinced me that I was unwanted, unlovable. I denied the reality that within me lived a young cis straight girl who had been running the show from behind the scenes for a long time, from within the shadows cast by the sweet elephant I loved. As long as I fed and cared for this elephant and reinforced my walls, I would never have to acknowledge her.

Could it really be that I believed this little idea that marriage would fix me? How embarrassing! So unrevolutionary! So not radically queer! But also, please love me?

What if I hadn't queered marriage at all?

Roland Barthes speaks of myth as a form of language, one that uses words, objects, and symbols to convey meaning. Myths arise out of social, cultural, and historical contexts, which means they can evolve through interaction and over time. I think often about the myth of marriage, the one that tugged me into its embrace in 2014 when I decided to legally jump in. What was the meaning I was chasing?

Writing has been a form of both resistance and resilience for me, since I first was able to string words together into a story on a page. Words are portals that teach me to traverse dimensions, to encounter sentience in its many forms, and to travel with the ancestors. They have invited me to dream; they have taught me how to swim with sharks and how to break bread with wolves. The words that move through me are often not mine, or not mine alone. They are the acorns left at an altar by a devout squirrel, and they are the feathers of a songbird sacrificed at my feet. I am both word and meaning, the myth and the primordial soup underneath.

Yet, as my marriage was unraveling, I found it harder and harder to find words to express what was happening to me. I reached for them in the places I always knew them to be, and more and more often, I would come back empty-handed. Words used to spill freely out of me, rolling off my skin, the fingers and tendrils of mycelium that kept me connected to life itself. But now, where were they? What was it that I couldn't say? Everything had dried up, nothing felt alive anymore. Were my words truly lost or simply hiding from me?

There is a loneliness in losing oneself. Without my words, would I be able to survive?

As I began to acknowledge the elephant in the room, and began to say hello to my many seemingly impenetrable walls, they did something weird. My walls began to reveal doors within them, ones I would slowly learn how to open—some with keys, others with ancient incantations the cells in my body would invoke. The antidote to shame is nonjudgment, or rather, compassionate curiosity. My words began to gently reappear. Perhaps they had been waiting for the right time to come out of hiding.

What else might be residing in the shadows? The elephant invited me to sit down with her, and when I did, we got to know each other so much better. She showed me her secrets, and I whispered my fears into her enormous ears. And we sat. She wove stories for me and rethreaded memories from the past to the present. Here we were, two misunderstood beings holding space for each other, vibrating with the stillness of the earth, coming alive at the bursting seams of rebirth. We were falling in love.

It would take almost six years for me to hear the one story she so patiently kept safe for me, waiting for the time when I would be ready to hear it.

The elephant asked me, "Remember the prayer you uttered as you cried at your altar that one day—the day you knew for certain that the marriage was over?"

"May we both be free," I whispered back. "Yes, I do remember."

I had shackled myself to the myth that love and marriage were intertwined, that by getting married, I would be loved in a way that would heal all my attachment wounds. I believed that marriage could save me, that it would finally tell me I was good enough. Marriage didn't make my parents love me more. Marriage didn't make me feel more safe. Marriage didn't give my younger self the assurance that they were begging for, that they were okay. Instead, my anxieties exploded and my confidence crumbled.

I was far from being free.

In *Borderlands/La Frontera: The New Mestiza*, Gloria Anzaldúa writes about creating a new mythos as a process through which we are able to shift perceptions of reality and of ourselves. It is a discovery of the not-yet-imagined, and it is where one might locate the space to breathe and exist. I hear in her discourse that a new mythos carries within it the potential for getting free. As I wander through the aftermath of divorce (in the different forms in which I have lived it), I wonder how the new words emerging can be used to write a new mythos of love, for myself. Marriage and love are not synonymous. They can and do coexist, but their coexistence is not a given, automatic thing. Divorce is not a failure to love and be loved. I am still awkwardly wading through that lesson.

To extract or disconnect meaning from an object or idea is a complicated task. Perhaps it is a kind of surgery, a restructuring and reimagining of what was. Perhaps it is a return to the essence of a sacred thing in a form I have not encountered before.

What is the liberatory shape of marriage, of divorce? For me, divorce has been an invitation to redefine love for myself and others as a practice of liberation. It tore me apart both times (financially, physically, spiritually, and emotionally), and it demanded that I dream bigger. It taught me that if my prayer for queer liberation—and with it, a prayer for the liberation of all beings—is to be realized, a new mythos of love is desperately needed.

The day my divorce was finalized, a queer friend asked me, "What was the biggest lesson you learned from this?"

"Marriage is overrated," I replied.

Through the cynicism of my response I reheard the wise admonition in the words my Taiwanese grandmother had spoken to me more than a decade earlier, after my grandfather passed away: "Don't get married." She gently placed my hand in hers. "You need to be free."

I sat at my ancestor altar this morning and bowed to her. "*A-ma*. Yes, may we all be free."

The Dharma of Divorce

JACOBY BALLARD

One of my best friends, a couples therapist and divorcee herself, advised me, "Leave no stone unturned so that you have no regrets." This was before I broke up with my partner, but in the midst of things being exceedingly difficult between us. Over the course of two years, I followed my friend's advice: couples therapy, romantic date plans, nights away together without our child, ritualized conversations, and a fifteenth-anniversary trip to Yellowstone. Yet things did not shift between us. My grievances went unanswered or dodged, my needs unmet. I heard from fellow divorcees that "when you know, you know." So I continued pouring energy into the relationship until I just wanted out of it. One moment of clarity was my partner's birthday. Despite being a romantic person, I gave her no card or gift, for doing so would have felt inauthentic. I just didn't want to. We quarreled several times that night and the next morning, even though we had a night away from parenting and a delicious birthday meal. She wore a scant nightslip to bed, and I was just not interested. I was exhausted. I broke up with her three days later.

I have been studying the Buddhadharma since I was seventeen, and as a practitioner, I have come to see everything as dharma, an opportunity to see the truth, a teaching, a lesson. It could be present in the words of a postal clerk, on a billboard, in a Facebook post. This process of divorce has been deep dharma for the past year: my greatest teacher in what love is, and what it is not, in honoring my truth, in not taking on what is not mine, investing my energy with purpose and attention and divesting from my desire for the affirmation or understanding of my ex.

My ex and I were both dating other people through our divorce, and our outside relationships were shining lights on the gaps and limits of our relationship. We also both had intimate friendships where parts of us were held that couldn't be held by one another. I never expected her to hold all of me, to connect on every front, and in the actual divorce, my beloved community has held me. My other partner easily met my needs: I felt cherished and respected, desired and reciprocated. She asked me, "In a spiritual sense, why are you and Z together?" I answered, "To heal our trauma, and to coparent our child." Our trauma—plus the compounding factors of late-stage capitalism, the lack of community in Salt Lake City, and the global pandemic—was beyond what we could heal, though we really tried. In a rare and brief vulnerable moment after a couples therapy session, we cried together over how we had both really tried to make it work. I am grateful to polyamory; without it, I would have stayed, less aware of what I needed and wanted, and continuing tirelessly to try to make it work and bend myself around what my ex was actually capable of. And at the same time, at this moment, I am not sure I want to pursue polyamory now, as I was disappointed and betrayed through that experience.

In this life, I have been fired for being trans, experienced health care discrimination, carried and birthed a baby as a transmasculine person, been uninvited from blood-family gatherings, experienced fracture in queer and organizing communities, faced the loss of a community organization that I cofounded, and moved to different states many times, starting over in community and work. Divorce is the most difficult thing I have faced in my adult life. There is complexity and nuance, hurt and disappointment between my ex and me, and I have no interest in airing details publicly; that doesn't serve anyone's healing or evolution, which is what I am most committed to. My hope has been that our shared community could stick by us both through a moment of pain, without cementing into stories of blame. I see this as a moment for my ex and me to heal, grow, and experience delight and joy as human beings less tethered to one another. We will always be connected because we are raising a child together, but this fifteen-year chapter of being beloveds, partners on the path of life, and each other's best friend has come to an end. Everything that has a beginning has an ending. I am grateful for these years together, and I am ready for what is next, the many possibilities.

I did everything I could to preserve my relationship. I really wanted to be one of the few queer couples that grows into old age together, outlasting all others. At ten years, we already were that. At fifteen, we were an anomaly. And that was the end of the road for us. When I told my colleague La Sarmiento the news, they asked, "Who said that longevity is the marker of a meaningful relationship?" I continue to reflect on that in what I move into now. What do I want? What is meaningful, what is success, what is integrity, what feels good? These are such important questions, and for the last two years of my relationship, I had stopped asking them.

My ex and I remain the parents of our child with 50/50 custody, though I wouldn't call what we are doing coparenting. We "parallel parent," with some degree of consistency for our child. Occasionally, particularly during crises, we collaborate; but mostly we just make our own decisions and inform each other of our child's state of being when we hand her off to the other parent: body, activities, school, sleep. There is much that I don't know about my child's life with my ex, and much I don't share with my ex about our papa-kiddo relationship. I've become a better parent through separation, more confident in my parenting choices and more connected to my child.

I have wondered about the promise and perils of legal queer marriage. We got legally married nine years into our relationship to protect my partner's relationship as the nongestational parent with our child who was then on the way in the red state of Utah. What did I really gain from legal marriage? In some ways, it has made my breakup more of a hassle to legally disentangle. In other ways, I feel grateful for the blueprint of navigating a breakup with assets and a child protected by divorce law. I wouldn't trust my ex to be fair and gracious without the protection of the law. As a queer and trans person, living in this age of unprecedented numbers of laws against queer and trans people, I know that laws are a tool that can be used to help or to harm.

Oh, the law. My ex wanted to navigate separation without lawyers, to trust one another as we unraveled, as all the feelings about what didn't work in our relationship were front and center. I knew that I had bent to her will for so long in our relationship, acquiescing again and again, that I needed backup, someone whom I paid to be my advisor and advocate. For much of my life, I have become accustomed to making things work, disregarding my needs and preferences in the process, and I certainly did that in my relationship with my ex. My ex was furious when I chose to use a lawyer, charging that I wasn't living up to our abolitionist politics and that I was pursuing a "straight" divorce. The end result is that even with a lawyer, I did not receive some of what I wanted in the division of things. If I had not had a lawyer, I would have lost much, much more.

The mocking of my choice as a "straight divorce" was reminiscent of familiar judgment that can fill queer spaces, whether someone is down, woke, aware, or not. A purity politic in which we police our borders fiercely and sometimes remove one another. I had not thought that my ex would stoop to questioning my queerness because of how I was pursuing separation, but through this divorce, again and again, she expressed her grief and rage through a political analysis of my behavior, with terms like "gendered labor" or a judgment of me "abandoning my purported class politics" when I followed up on our agreed-upon payout from the house. It's a familiar move among queer folks—calling upon our politics when we feel vulnerable. I can look back into our relationship to see this pattern there, and I wish we had both turned toward vulnerability rather than relying on the armor of progressive politics; yet another learning in the dharma of divorce.

We didn't ever believe that marriage marked our relationship as valid or differentiated how we were together before being legally married. I wanted a commitment ceremony for the majority of our fifteen years together, and we never had one. My ex didn't want to pay the costs involved and said that money could be better funneled toward social justice causes. I wanted a ritual marking, to call in community as witness so the people around us could commit to us as a couple, supporting us individually and collectively. When we legally married in 2018, we were clear that marriage was a tool, not an identity. She would call me her husband only when it was protecting me or our relationship. Otherwise, we referred to each other as beloveds and partners, and we spoke of our “partnership” rather than our marriage. And yet, when we split retirement accounts, she insisted that we only do so beginning from 2018, when we were married, which is what the law requires. When marriage mattered materially, she recognized it as a marker.

In the midst of my breakup with my partner, the person I was dating—the illuminating and validating sweetheart that I had—broke up with me because there was not enough room for our relationship to be the sacred connection that it was within the narrow confines of my marriage. She was committed to her own dignity and well-being, and she knew she could not be well and dignified within what was available within my partnership. Going through two breakups at once that spring felt particularly queer. The layers of heartbreak were part of every waking breath for months. I couldn’t sleep thinking that in my efforts to stay with my partner, I had lost my soulmate. For months I had nightmares, aware of the layers of pain and incompatibility within my partnership that had been unbearable to recognize within the relationship. A good friend and dharma teacher offered two useful tools. First, she said, “Some days I just go to bed early, putting an end to a hard day.” She also offered a reframe on the suffering and enormous tasks in divorce: the possibility that “maybe this is the best thing that ever happened to me.” This allowed me to see possibility on the other side of emotionally laden tasks, and to look for the goodness, rather than dwell in shame, disappointment, and grief.

Holding two simultaneous breakups brought clarity. One was a profound loss of so much unexplored territory and precious divine connection, the other a grief for how the relationship had deteriorated and the disappointment in the promise of longevity in being “life partners.” I was ready to let go of and be released from one of these relationships, having turned over every stone. The other I was attached to, curious about, feeling more seen, valued, playful, and met than ever before. Months later, after I had left my partner, we reconnected, our love undeniable and enduring, and now we have all the room we need to build a relationship that we each want, without the input or influence of someone else.

Divorce has been a spiritual process, and I now have a sangha (beloved community) of friends who have gone through it. They have held me, guided me, asked important questions, and reflected back to me what they were seeing and who they know me to be. They have offered a read on my ex, protective of me and my tendency to acquiesce and comply with my ex's demands and desires. They helped me gain steady footing and awareness of dynamics at play so I wouldn't betray myself to please her. I have learned that my friends, my chosen family, those are the lasting partnerships wherein we don't negotiate schedules, parenting, finances in the same way; rather, we have an enduring and committed relationship with one another that has outlasted sexual and romantic partnerships.

Before conception, my ex and I had imagined our child being held by an enormous community. Then we moved across the country, leaving behind our most precious people. We were consumed by newborn life six months after arriving in Utah, and the pandemic isolated us further. In this moment, it feels like our divorce has offered that broad community to our child: more grown-ups consistently in her life (partners, roommates, colleagues, beloveds who are closer now), caring for her deeply, inspiring different parts of her to emerge than was previously possible within our isolated nuclear family during the pandemic. We wouldn't have imagined that a separation would bring our child more deeply into a beloved community, but it undeniably has, and I am grateful. Our child doesn't have the two-parent home that she had for five years, but she has two homes free of the tension that previously pervaded our home. My ex and I support one another's parenting relationship with our child, but otherwise we do not interact. This is how it is right now, less than a year out, and it might change over time. As a queer person, I always imagine becoming friends upon a breakup, but it hasn't happened here thus far despite continuing to share something precious: our child.

Gay marriage *can* be a spiritual commitment and process as well, but the institution of marriage is not necessary for a spiritual partnership. I feel relieved to have some legal processes in place that my ex and I don't have to create together, that we are beholden to because we were married. Through this process, I have come to respect the utility of laws and lawyers in a way that I hadn't previously, having navigated a profound life shift with someone who didn't want it and painted me as the villain. However, I still do not think that laws will set us free. Laws follow the tides of the citizens: Women weren't allowed to vote until they demanded it; civil rights legislation didn't pass until decades of organizing had shifted public opinion. I do not think same-sex marriage being legal grants queer folks freedom, although at the same time I am grateful for a long-standing history of divorce law anticipating what my ex and me brought to the table. A legal divorce has reinforced an embrace of nuance and complexity.

I stepped out of a vortex, having been so influenced by my ex's needs, preferences, and perspectives. Now I get to create the life I want, unbeholden to anyone else. In the three years since my divorce I have hiked more than I have in the six years I've lived in Utah. I meditate every morning and every night, either chanting with my child in my lap or in quiet solitude when she is with her other parent. I have gone to more concerts and made more medicine and foods from the plants grown on the land I now steward than I did previously. I have come to value myself, to honor my needs and desires as valid, important, and relevant, and to be a partner unto myself. I have become a better parent, fully present with my child when I am with her, and practicing rituals of connection and care while resourcing myself deeply on days when I don't have custody.

I walk into the queer bookstore where I live in Salt Lake City, and I find a card that reads: "You have really ruined the sanctity of marriage now: Congratulations on your divorce." This card was written for queer folks, with "really" written in rainbow colors. I chuckle; I am recognized in this dharma of divorce.

Praying for the Strength of a Hummingbird

TAHNIE HOLCOMB

Author's note: My ex-spouse and I both use they/them pronouns.

On the day when I thought I was going to be punched while holding our toddler, I knew I had to seek separation. As my spouse lunged at me, pupils wide with rage, I felt my body shaking and our two-year-old's body shaking. "You're an abusive motherfucker," I heard myself hiss in a low voice. I was shocked to hear that word "abusive" leave my mouth for the first time in the six years of the relationship. I also felt a deep knowing in my belly that it was true.

Scenes began to flash through my mind in seconds: images of being blocked in rooms or body-checked by my partner, who is taller and stronger than I am; one episode of explosive rage after another, where they would quickly act as if nothing had happened and almost seem cheerful where I was left drained and sad; times of recovering from surgery when I'd be left alone after being told they'd spend a few days with me to help me, such as the time I fell on the floor the day after a major surgery while trying to heat up some soup and was unable to get up by myself, so I lay there in pain for hours until they came home; being yelled at or talked to in a hateful voice in front of our toddler; the multiple times I made dinner for the three of us and then waited hours past the agreed-upon time for my spouse to come home, who said they'd been catching up with a friend or had stayed late at a work event; being told I should stop wearing a certain pair of shorts because "you've gained weight and they're not attractive anymore"; early memories of our dating, when I found out that they'd lied about the nature of a so-called platonic friendship and their financial situation. Hundreds of moments flooded my mind as I realized I had made a serious mistake in staying in this relationship. I come from a lineage with a lot of domestic violence and its long-term impacts on the family, so on that day when I thought my spouse was going to punch me with our toddler in my arms, my wise self told me: "I can't raise our child witnessing this for one more day." It wasn't until later, months and months after leaving, that I could also hear the part of me that said: "*I* don't deserve this treatment for one more day."

At first I thought there would be a way for couples counseling to help us chart a new path to staying together. Only a few sessions into it, the words I was hearing in the sessions made very clear to me that the only option was permanent separation. Despite how painful the past few years had been in the relationship, I still had to process my grief. I was grieving a dream of what I thought my life was going to be like and the family structure I wanted my child to have. I was also grieving the fact that I would not be living in the house we had recently bought, where my dog had just been buried in the yard.

At first, I had some naive belief that we could coparent collaboratively, and maybe even someday be friends. I suggested a "kitchen table" meeting at a diner to talk about a parenting and separation agreement. Just a few minutes into the conversation, I realized that we were coming to the conversation with very different goals and desires. I said that because of our child, we would always be family and that it'd be best for our child if we could collaborate. My child's other parent said coldly, "You're not my family." It felt like a gut punch. A chill went down my neck when my ex looked in my eyes with no expression and flatly said, "There are consequences to leaving me." I knew it wasn't good, but had I known what was going to transpire after that, I would have made a lot of concrete plans in advance. I had no idea the "consequences" of leaving were going to be immense—emotionally, financially, and socially.

At first, I told mutual friends very little about the reason for our separation, saying there was "too much conflict" or that "there are things I don't want to talk about." I told friends who were close to me, and not my ex, about the dynamics of the relationship over the years, and they were supportive. But once I realized that my ex had no desire to coparent or create a fair divorce agreement, I knew I had to seek legal counsel. Prior to our court-required mediation,

I was contacted by the court coordinator, who referred me to a domestic violence (DV) survivor's program and expressed concern for my safety. They said they would only conduct the mediation session online with us in two separate Zoom rooms for safety reasons.

Due to my ex's irrational and sometimes threatening behavior, and because the court coordinator expressed her concerns for my safety, I started to fear that my ex would severely hurt me or both me and our child. I told my closest circle that if anything happened to me, they should know it was my ex, and I started working on a will and trust for my child (with the help of an old friend, who is an incredible queer attorney). I got an alarm system for my apartment and, at the suggestion of the DV case manager, a window ladder, since we lived on the second floor. After it was court-ordered that our parenting time exchanges happen in the school parking lot, I noticed that my ex would park as far away as possible from the front of the school where the school's cameras were, so I got a dash cam in case anything went awry at an exchange. Now, two years after the separation, still waiting for finalization of the divorce, my ex has been seen in the parking lot of my workplace near my car. I'm not sure I'll ever be able to relax about this. All my research on narcissistic abuse over the past two years has shown I should probably stay vigilant. Studies show that people with high levels of narcissistic traits fixate on former partners they perceive as rejecting them, which can lead to behaviors such as excessive communication, stalking, or attempts to control the former partner.*

About six months after we separated, I started to notice that some mutual friends had distanced themselves from me or even completely stopped speaking to me. This was another thing I had to grieve. I am heartbroken to discover that people who I thought knew me—truly knew me, for years—would not reach out to check on me or ask to talk to me about my concerns regarding

* J. R. Meloy, ed., *The Psychology of Stalking: Clinical and Forensic Perspectives* (Academic Press, 2001); Manya Wakefield, "Stalking and Narcissistic Personality Disorder," Narcissistic Abuse Rehab, March 16, 2025, www.narcissisticabuserehab.com/stalking-and-narcissistic-personality-disorder/; Nicholas J. S. Day, Michelle L. Townsend, and Brin F. S. Grenyer, "Pathological Narcissism: An Analysis of Interpersonal Dysfunction Within Intimate Relationships," *Personality and Mental Health* 16, no. 3 (2022): 204–16, www.doi.org/10.1002/pmh.1532.

what my ex might have said. I started to see how queer circles seemed to prioritize marriages and couples, and I felt very isolated and alone. I saw how people were probably acting on assumptions and maybe personal biases instead of trying to ascertain all the facts or all perspectives. It was a hard realization and lesson for me. And, to be real, it led to some disillusionment I have with the queer "left," many of whom say they understand intimate partner violence (IPV) but have no concept of covert abuse and postseparation abuse. I think there are some who don't care, and some who are engaging in their own forms of abuse behind closed doors. That broke my heart more than losing the marriage.

I was dealing with verbal abuse, financial abuse, and DV by proxy (abuse using our child as a weapon) for months on end. Meanwhile, my ex was a director of a local nonprofit, going out and about to queer and trans events and speaking at events around the country while sending private messages to me making transphobic statements related to our child and myself. It was such a mindfuck. For a year or more, I felt like I'd lost myself, my reality, my community, and my faith in other people. Nothing I'd seen in the folks doing transformative justice work in our community gave me any confidence that they could handle something like this, especially since many don't want to consider the specifics of personality disorders or subtypes of narcissistic abuse due to rejecting the Western conceptualizations found in the *DSM-V*. I understand those thoughts and viewpoints about diagnoses, and maybe I even used to share some of them; but both my experience and the knowledge I have of hundreds of nearly identical stories of other survivors has taught me otherwise. It seems almost impossible to me to effectively intervene in postseparation abuse and covert abuse without a foundation of understanding how some personality disorders manifest. Additionally, the community cohesion needed to implement the intensive mechanisms of accountability necessary to curtail narcissistic abuse doesn't seem to exist at this point in time.

I had to turn to the family court system, which I'd never imagined myself entering and didn't know much about. It was my last resort to seek some measure of peace for myself and safety for my child. As with the other court systems, I learned how messed up and brutal that court system is. I still had to accept that it was my only chance to secure some measure of safety and stability.

I also lost my grandmother during that time. She was the only immediate family member who I was close with and still spoke to me. She was a DV survivor, and I knew that it was crucial for ancestral healing that I do whatever I had to do to break this cycle.

Fortunately, I found two therapists—one a talk therapist, and the other an Indigenous somatics therapist—who both had a lot of knowledge about DV, IPV, and personality disorders. Those two, and my handful of friends who knew everything that was going on behind the scenes, somehow kept me functioning during this time. That and my deep, deep love for my child.

During this time I began working as a therapist again, and on various other projects and DEI contracts. I was still mostly able to show up in real time at work as I wanted, but my anxiety and the pressure of having to manage logistics and finances for my child and myself while working full time made my thoughts scattered. It felt like my brain was overflowing with details, and I dropped balls on work projects. I generally felt a lot of shame about appearing unreliable or flaky to people and groups I cared about. I literally had no capacity to do otherwise. I really felt like I shouldn't be trying to work at all, but I had no financial way to take time off. I had to file bankruptcy due to the financial abuse I received from my ex, and I was forced to move my child and myself into a shared one-bedroom apartment for the duration of the divorce process.

I kept taking it one day at a time. I was willing to use any coping mechanism possible to help me stay alive and fight my way out of a deep hole. I was working all the hours I could during day care hours, and I had no time for exercise, which was usually a form of stress relief. Instead, I was smoking a lot of cigarettes and eating a lot of sugar, and for three months, I received ketamine treatment for PTSD symptoms. I remember thinking that my therapy clients and others who knew me would be so disappointed at how I was coping with the stress. I continued to tell myself that I needed to do whatever it took to survive in that time period, until the final court hearing was over and I could start to rebuild some financial stability and stop being flooded by cortisol every week when dealing with my ex's latest antics.

I was forty-six years old and felt in so many ways that I was starting over in life. I am a twice-published author, a therapist with a fifteen-year career, and a public speaker. As stable as I felt my career and income were, the divorce process threatened my livelihood. Throughout the divorce, I was relying on food banks for groceries, and I received financial support from a group of friends who called themselves my Carebears. I really think the Carebears kept me afloat during that time period, and I'm forever grateful.

And in some ways, with everything I'd lost, I gained so much. The time I spent sharing a small space (and a bed) with my child from ages two to four was a blessing. I felt that at the end of our long work days and day care days, and especially after coming back together after separation, snuggling at night gave us both a needed comfort and reassurance.

Losing so much financially highlighted for me the things that really mattered. The experience proved that my home can be cozy and soothing, even when it's small and overflowing with kids' toys and art. I appreciated what I did have. I appreciated the ability to keep my thermostat set to a comfortable temperature for my body, to choose whether or not to listen to music, to have people over or not, to keep my child on their routine in my home, to have a peaceful home. The summer after separating, the crepe myrtle outside my balcony fed so many hummingbirds. I hadn't seen them like that in years, and I felt like they were coming to that tree to reassure me with their small, mighty, swift, and beautiful bodies. I would stand and watch them, and I would say hello to them, these winged relatives. They reminded me of my grandmother who had died that year, because she always fed hummingbirds at her house. I thought maybe she had sent them.

Through the steadfast love of a handful of my friends and community members and my deep healing work in therapy, I began to slowly rebuild my confidence and trust in myself and my intuition. I gained so much clarity about what I want within all of my relationships, and about what I can no longer accept. This clarity has, at times, been painful, especially when it meant certain relationships needed to change or end. It has also felt very freeing. It has felt good to find love for myself. I know I'll have to be aware of the wounds that led me to accept mistreatment at different points in my life so I can check myself if I start to slip into self-betrayal.

Through the postseparation abuse and realization of all the ways our child was being used as a form of punishment or control, despite the negative impacts on her emotionally, I gained an even stronger commitment to parenting during my custodial time. I want to teach my child any wisdom I've inherited and learned, using modeling, words and stories, and relationships with members of my community who care about my child's well-being. I know this is the most important thing I am called to do at this point in my life. I have to be a safe and peaceful place for my child who will likely be experiencing really hard things 50 percent of the time in her other home. My body went through four years of in vitro fertilization while I strove to become a parent, and I don't take it lightly that this desire came to fruition. It is a joyous responsibility. It's the most emotionally, physically, and spiritually challenging thing I've ever done, and at the same time, it's the most intense love I've ever felt.

This is why it was so heart-wrenchingly painful to see how our child was suffering and feel helpless to stop it. Early on in the separation, there were times when our two-year-old would start taking all her clothes off or run and hide in the closet when it was time to leave to go to the other parent, or would hide behind me at the exchange. She had intense tantrums, screaming for twenty minutes straight. She bit multiple children and teachers at day care for months on end. Today, at age four, our child has a lot more vocabulary, and I've worked hard to make sure she has words for a range of feelings. After a few recent months of peace, our child has started to struggle again. She's been acting out aggressively at school, throwing big tantrums, and having bedwetting accidents again. This coincides with her repeatedly saying she doesn't want to go to the other house and she wants to stay with me. She recently asked, "Who do I have to tell that I don't want to go there who won't make me go?" This is heartbreaking every time. It goes against everything I feel in my core about my role as a parent. Recently, I was able to get her into play therapy for support, but I know that this comes with risks. My ex does not want her in therapy and could use that in court against me, to accuse me of making legal decisions they don't agree with.

Several times during the marriage, I told my spouse that the relationship felt chaotic and that it was the most chaotic relationship I'd ever been in. Her response was that our relationship was normal. At the time, gaslighting had so overrun my intuition—and I had ignored it so much—that my immediate response was to doubt myself and believe the relationship must be normal after all. What I've learned since then is that chaos, unpredictability, and instability are hallmarks of narcissistic abuse, as are intentional strategies to keep the target off-center and doubting their own judgment. I remember telling my therapist a year before separation that I didn't understand why I always felt confused in the relationship. I now know that feeling that degree of confusion is an intentional outcome of the abuse, sown through circular arguments, the devaluing phase that follows love-bombing, "bread-crumbing," the "word salad" answers to questions, and so many other behaviors that create massive confusion and avoidance of bringing up any requests or possible topics of disagreement.

I started connecting with other survivors of covert narcissistic abuse and learning strategies for managing some of the behaviors. I began to learn some of the boundaries I could request via court order to try to minimize some of the emotional abuse and my ex's use of our child as a pawn. I was also learning that the court would not prioritize my boundaries as an IPV survivor. Due to our shared custody, I would be at risk of engaging with my ex in ways that would not feel comfortable. I knew I needed an attorney who understood IPV and narcissistic personality disorder. I did more research and switched to a new attorney. I needed somebody who didn't play, and in our first meeting I could tell she understood the dynamics more than others did.

While I would never wish my experience with this divorce on anyone (and I know I will always be navigating my ex's behaviors), after a couple of years I feel like I'm getting reacquainted with my true self and getting to know the new self I am now. I feel like I'm finally, on some cellular level, believing in the type of treatment I deserve and the types of love I deserve. In some ways, getting back in touch with my own wisdom and intuition feels incredibly liberating. I'm fiercely devoted to protecting my peace that feels hard won. It's not easy at this point envisioning what my life may look like five years from now. I'm comfortable with that because I'm good with me.

After starting my queer separation at age forty-four, I don't intend to ever marry again. My divorce has taken over two years to finalize through the legal system. It has cost over $40,000 and counting in attorney fees and court fees; has catapulted me into bankruptcy, despite the fact that I'm working full time with a decent salary; and has been an extremely emotionally stressful and painful process after only a six-year marriage.

I've examined the reasons why I wanted to be married, and I understand how it was connected to being rejected by my biological family. I wanted to create my own nuclear family so I would always have people who loved me. Allowing myself time to heal and be single gave me the space to observe how ingrained heteronormativity is, even within queer and trans communities, where couples and nuclear two-parent families with children are seen as signs of health and success. Other queer couples distanced themselves from me, as if divorce might be contagious. Being legally married to another nonbinary person legitimized my queer relationship in broader society, too. I felt as if people accepted us as more "normal," and other married couples, including straight, cis couples, could relate to us as a married couple. Saying "spouse" to other people got a different reaction from all the times I've said "partner." I don't hear queer communities talk about this much. It's like we think we've evolved past this in our beliefs without examining our actions. Now, as a single parent, there are times I feel more understood by straight single parents than by queer people.

Going through the family court system to establish custody agreements and child support is a scary process as a trans, queer person who raised a child from birth without assigning the child a gender. Prior to becoming pregnant, my ex and I had been on the same page about not assigning a gender to our child. When our three-year-old started verbalizing one gender (and not expressing it in stereotypical ways with clothing), my ex started to accuse me of coaching our child to talk that way. I was terrified by the possibility of my ex leveraging the court system's transphobia to take my child away from me. I also feared for my child's emotional well-being if her other parent was not going to take the path of validating her verbalized gender identity. This was a scenario I never, ever predicted prior to separating from this person, and it was just one more example highlighting the abuse I'd endured in the relationship and that our child had been exposed to. I found that very few people in my queer community could understand this. I was very isolated, having very few empathetic people to talk to about what I was experiencing. The support groups I found were all straight, cis people. My queer friends generally had never seen or heard of anything like this.

I learned that I can create family for myself in all sorts of ways and that adoptive family relationships and close friendships brought me as much joy and connection as a romantic partner did. In some ways, I have more freedom to live my life in the way that feels best for me and my parenting style. I had the time to really think about what types of romantic and sexual relationship structures are going to work the best for my current life situation and to know that this might change as I continue to age and move through other phases of life. I'm noticing a lot of lightness with this feeling, as opposed to the past, when I felt some fear about being single for long stretches of time or worried about whether I would find a life partner. I'm not saying I never feel lonely or wish some things were different, but I don't think that finding a spouse or a monogamous or nesting partner is going to create satisfaction and happiness in my life. I understand that contentment, peace, and joy are feelings I can appreciate in all kinds of circumstances.

While watching cartoons with my child, this form of media constantly reminds me that children are inundated with messages that the two-parent household is the accurate family structure, and that the most important relationship is the one with a spouse. I see my four-year-old internalizing this messaging, which is also reinforced in preschool. I want to model something different for her. I know there are so many kinds of love, and I feel sad that we restrict ourselves to prioritizing one relationship and one type of love. Capitalism definitely reinforces the benefit of dual-income homes. I'm not going to lie: Sometimes I wish I was sharing life expenses with somebody else. At the same time, sharing household bills and intertwining finances ended up putting me in the most precarious financial situation I've been in since my late teens and early twenties, so I don't plan on doing that again.

The other way that marriage felt like a requirement was that in the state I lived in while starting my fertility journey, I had to be married for at least six months to be considered a legal parent of my child. I'm so grateful that I had the foresight to legally adopt our child through a "second parent adoption" right after birth. I have no doubt that my ex would have challenged my parental rights after separation without it.

I'm currently sitting on a cozy leather couch in a satin robe, holding a glass of wine and looking out at the Sandia Mountains where I'm visiting my adoptive family, as my child sleeps in the bedroom. Her sleeping face is one of the most beautiful things I've ever seen, and the fullness in my heart when I look at her is both ecstatic and painful. I just had a phone conversation with a close friend, dreaming up a trip we may take together, talking about a couple of crushes I have and my friend's new apartment. I've been enjoying figuring out what my sexuality looks like now as a tired primary parent who works a lot and also really likes sex. In this new life of mine there are hard days, lonely days, along with loud laughter, hugs, dancing, connection, deep talks, woods walks, shared meals, shared fears and desires, and a commitment to the child part of me who wants and deserves care. I realize now that because of our shared child, I can never really escape my ex. I can never really leave or stop the abuse. That is a terrible thing to know. I also know that I won't let that stop me from loving our child, myself, and other people in the fiercest ways I can. That particular freedom makes me think of the hummingbirds and smile.

No Good Deed

PAUL A. AGUILAR

We met online six months after my breakup with Peter, whom I had been with for exactly seven and a half years. Exactly. To the hour, almost. No joke. Peter, thirteen years my junior, and I ended our romantic entanglement in the spring of 2004. That was when I discovered online dating sites. They were still in their infancy, but they were a great alternative to going to bars. I also became very adept at online flirtation and fantasy.

On one of those sites, I met David. Truth be told, David was a total contradiction of what I normally found attractive and interesting. Our mutual love of live theater was what we first bonded over. We would spend hours chatting online or texting about our favorite shows, actors, directors, producers, costume designers, lighting designers, set designers, and so on. We loved discussing what TV show or movie we thought would make a great Broadway show and who we would cast in it.

The two of us messaged back and forth for several months before we met face to face. During that time, I shared that I had recently ended a long-term relationship and was finding it difficult to be a forty-plus-year-old, recently dumped, HIV-positive, gay male who didn't drink or do drugs. When he asked about my favorite pastimes, my answer was simple: If I wasn't ushering at theaters showing productions that were part of San Francisco's Best of Broadway series, working out at the Civic Center YMCA, or using my BowFlex in my apartment, then I could be found hanging out with my nephews, who were ages five and nine at the time.

David shared that he was new to San Francisco and that he and his two adopted sons had just moved here from Pennsylvania. The boys, ages ten and eleven, were attending Harvey Milk Civil Rights Academy where David was volunteering to help produce the annual school musical, a junior version of *Pippin*.

After months and months of online flirting, we finally set a date to meet in person: January 1, 2005. I was to come out to their home in the Richmond district for a New Year's Day dinner and meet his sons. He and his ex had adopted them through the New York state foster care program. After dinner, we planned to watch one of the *Star Wars* movies recently released on DVD, which I insisted on bringing, along with dessert. The evening went well. The boys were on their best behavior and full of questions about San Francisco and about me and my life. The moment I met these boys, I knew I was meant to be in their lives.

As the evening progressed, I began to learn a little more of their backstory and how they ended up in San Francisco. The story, as it was told to me, was that David's ex, Keith, insisted on moving out here after coming home from work one night claiming they were being watched and that there were cameras in the trees that surrounded their home in a rural gated community in Milford, Pennsylvania (or, as I like to call it, "Pennsyltucky"). So, David, Keith, and the boys, Tiberius and Allard, drove across the country with all they could fit into David's little Nissan Cube and landed in San Francisco.

A few months following their arrival, Keith's behavior became erratic. He would disappear for days at a time; when he returned, he would be irritated and would lock himself in the bedroom to sleep for days on end, leaving David to handle all the important details such as finding a more permanent place to live, figuring out where the boys should attend school, and so on. The stress of the drive across the country and the lack of support David was getting from Keith took its toll on David's health, and as a result, David became very ill and landed in the hospital. Initially, David thought it was just exhaustion. He hadn't been eating right or sleeping properly during the cross-country drive. When they arrived in San Francisco, he started to feel as though he might have the flu. When he almost collapsed one afternoon when picking the boys up from class, Keith insisted he go to the hospital. A round of tests came back indicating that David was positive for HIV and hepatitis C. Following this discovery, Keith discovered that he, too, had become HIV positive. Keith announced that he had decided San Francisco wasn't the place for him, and he was going to stay with his parents in Connecticut and start a new life there, leaving David, Tiberius, and Allard stranded in San Francisco. Shortly after that, I came on the scene.

David started on HIV meds as well as hepatitis C treatment, which involved infusions every two weeks. After his infusions, he would stop by my studio apartment and spend the afternoon fitfully sleeping in my arms until it was time to get the boys from school. I'd been diagnosed HIV positive in 1988, so I was familiar with all the public health resources available to people living with HIV in San Francisco, and I proceeded to get David connected to those services. After three months of treatment, he had cleared the hep C virus. It was about that time that Keith decided that he was unhappy in Connecticut. One evening, David called me quite agitated and told me Keith had returned to San Francisco. Keith had somehow managed to pay for a flight from Connecticut to Oakland International Airport. Keith had told David he wanted to get back together and try to work on himself, their relationship, and their family. David confessed to me that he wasn't sure of how to proceed; apparently Keith had made promises like this in the past and had never been able to keep them. David was also concerned that Keith was far too involved with his crystal meth addiction and that he was just being manipulative. David asked for my advice.

Well, I'm no homewrecker, and I believe that any attempt to put a family back together is worth a shot, so I offered David the following advice: If Keith was committed to everything he told David, then David should have Keith meet him at a Narcotics Anonymous meeting, which happened to be scheduled for that very evening at 8:00 p.m., not far from the 16th Street BART station. "By meeting you at the meeting, at least you will know his desire to stop using is genuine," I explained. David said Keith had told him he had no way of getting from Oakland Airport to San Francisco. I reminded David that Keith had somehow found enough money to purchase a plane ticket from Connecticut to Oakland; he certainly could find a way to get the $3.80 fare to hop on BART. I even went so far as to offer to go to the meeting with David as a source of support. He declined. I told him to phone me in the morning and let me know the outcome.

In the morning, David called and told me that Keith didn't show up at the meeting; instead, he showed up at David's house and became very aggressive when David told him he couldn't stay with him and the boys. I asked David if Keith was high; David said he was. I asked how Keith was able to afford these drugs if he had left his job. David told me about the $1,200 a month they received from the state of New York's foster care system, which was a stipend they would receive for each boy until the boys reached the age of twenty-four. This stipend was New York's way of helping with the additional costs of families adopting from the foster care system. The catch was that the check was made out to Keith, and David never saw a penny of it. David had also expressed his fear that Keith might try to take the boys back to New York. At this point, I told David that it sounded to me like he would need to get custody of the boys and find a way to get New York City to make the checks out to him. A couple of phone calls later, we found a family law attorney willing to take the case. I later helped David prepare his case, and as luck would have it, he did get full custody and eventually got the stipend in his name.

That year was my forty-second birthday. On the day before, David threw a surprise party for me; he knew that I traditionally celebrated my birthday proper with my family because it also happened to fall on my parents' wedding anniversary, June 19. In attendance at this surprise soiree were all our mutual friends. It was quite a day with good food and good friends, and it was enjoyed by all. It was also an opportunity for us to see how our friends would interact. I was happy to see that they got along splendidly. That evening, I spent the night at David's house.

It was just barely after sunrise the next morning when the boys knocked on the bedroom door. "Come in," I called, rubbing the sleep from beneath my eyes. The door flew open and the boys bounded in, jumping on the bed, the dogs right behind them. "GOOOOD MORNING!" they shouted. "So, did ya do it yet?" they asked their dad conspiratorially.

David smiled and said, "I told you guys we would do it together, so no, I haven't. Should we do it now?"

"Yes!" Right now!" they squealed.

David reached into the drawer of his nightstand and retrieved a small, square, black velvet box. He handed me the box and said, "I was wondering if you would do me the honor of becoming my fiancé?" I was stunned. I certainly wasn't expecting a marriage proposal on my forty-second birthday, or on any day, to be honest. I had written off having a long-term lover after Peter and I broke up. I had given up on my dream of getting old with someone.

I looked at David, then at the boys. "Now boys," I said, "you know what this means if I say yes, right? It means I will move in with you all and that I will become a part of your lives as well. It doesn't mean I'm replacing your Papa"—that was their name for their other dad, Keith—"or anything like that. All it means is that you will have three gay white dads. Are you okay with that?"

"Yeah, we know," Allard said. "Daddy"—their name for David—"already talked to us about it. We talked about it and decided it was okay. The only question we have is, what are we gonna call you?"

I said, "Well, let's just start with Paul and work from there." Within the week I began the process of moving in with them and helping to build a blended family.

I had told David I didn't want to get in the way of him and Keith reconciling if that was on the table for them. David assured me that would never happen, but I always felt as though I was a fifth wheel. Whenever Keith was in town, we tried to be the "modern" family by inviting him over to a meal with us and the boys, but I still just felt like a fifth wheel.

We married on October 28, 2008. We had wanted to get married on January 5, 2009, the anniversary of our first meeting. As I am one who likes to be prepared, I had discovered that one could obtain a marriage license and have the ceremony up to ninety days afterward, and the license would still be valid. This was the same year that Proposition 8, the so-called California Marriage Protection Act, would be going into effect, thereby putting a hold on same-sex marriage until such time as the US Supreme Court would decide its fate. David and I happened to be near City Hall that day and ducked in simply to pay for a marriage license, having no intention of using it until early January. But, as luck would have it, the clerk at the desk informed us that the moratorium on same-sex marriages was going to take place in a week, and if we were interested, there was one appointment available that afternoon to get married by a justice of the peace. Otherwise, she cautioned, we would have to wait until the Supreme Court made their decision.

Well, I wasn't one to ignore a sign from the heavens (or so I thought), so we sped home, got into our tuxes, got a friend to agree to be a witness, and hoofed it back to City Hall. It only took two hours for us to be wed. I guess you could say we eloped. It was just David, me, our friend, and the justice of the peace. Alas, neither of our families were very supportive of this act of spontaneity. It was too soon, too fast, and raised so many questions: What did we really know about each other, what about the boys, were the boys okay with it, was I going to adopt the boys? David and I stood our ground. When my own adoptive mother said to me, "Well, you know, they aren't even *your* children," I hung up the phone and didn't speak to her again for almost a year. I also began to understand why David never lived closer than two thousand miles away from his family. Neither family understood boundaries. So we continued on, married this time, but with little support from family. We did, however, get support from a few friends.

Then David began disappearing for hours at a time. At first, his excuses sounded plausible: explanations like "the bus was late," "the bus broke down," or "I was halfway home and had to go back because I left something" at whatever appointment he claimed he was attending. And then one day, I decided to surprise him. It was a Saturday, and I had been scheduled to work both the entire matinee and the early shift of the evening performance of *Jersey Boys* at the Curran Theatre. When I arrived at the theater, the head usher, Diondra, told me she had overscheduled staff and asked if I'd be willing to just work the early shift of the matinee. I had been working every show for the past week, so I was happy to give up the rest of the shifts to a fellow usher. So, instead of heading home at 8:30 in the evening, I was heading home at 2:30 p.m. I was so excited because the boys were spending the weekend with Keith, and that meant David and I could have some alone time together.

When I arrived home, much to my surprise, David was nowhere to be found. I called his phone; no answer. I texted. No response. I figured he must be running errands and decided I would shower and then start dinner to have it all ready for us to enjoy upon his return home. As I was taking off my usher uniform, I noticed that David had left his laptop on and open. I am not usually a snoop, but something that day told me to see what was on the screen. And lo, when the screen saver stopped, David's laptop was open to Manhunt, a gay dating site. It was open to a profile of a couple in the East Bay looking for a third playmate.

I was stunned. David and I had had this conversation early on in our relationship with an understanding that, when it came to sex, expecting just one person to be your *everything* was unrealistic. The agreement was, yes, we could play with others, but only together as a couple, and only if we both agreed on the third playmate. He was clearly violating that arrangement. When I texted David with the fact that he had left his laptop on and open when he left the house, he quickly called me. I spat, "What the f*** is going on, David?" as I answered the phone with one hand while tossing toiletries and clothing into an overnight bag.

"Well, I was hoping you'd come join us," he said.

"Really, and how did you know I would be home early, huh?" Dead silence on the other end. "According to the time stamp, you left this house not thirty minutes after I left for work. You sure didn't waste any time, did you? Don't expect me to be here when you get home." And I hung up. I grabbed my laptop, phone charger, and duffel bag, and I headed out the door. I got into my car and drove to *mi abuelita*'s house on the other side of Golden Gate Park.

Mi abuelita, my father's mother, had been telling me she was becoming lonely. She had been alone in her house since my grandfather passed away, and she'd said how nice it would be if I could come visit more often and maybe stay a night or two. She was ninety-four years old at the time. I never went back to live with David.

Over the next two years, we tried to work things out. We engaged a family therapist to help us try to navigate the complexities of a blended family. The problem with that was that the boys didn't see it as their problem; they saw it as something the adults needed to figure out. In the beginning, David would come over to Abuela's, bringing our puppies, Lucky and Gina, with him to visit. Abuela loved animals. One or two nights a week, he and the boys would come over to enjoy a meal with Abuela and me. Abuela loved having the boys visit, and she adored them just as much as she did her other great-grandkids. Two nights a week, I spent the night at their place on the other side of the park. On those evenings, my father's sisters would spend the night with Abuela.

Eventually, Tiberius went to live with Keith in New York. His acting out had gotten completely out of control, escalating to the point that David and I (when I was sleeping there) had to install a deadbolt lock on the inside of our bedroom door. Why did we do that, you ask? Because one evening I awoke to find Tiberius with a baseball bat in his hands, swinging it at my head. Tiberius really wanted to be with Keith. By this time, Keith had very quickly pulled it together, gotten clean and sober, secured a teaching position with a New York private school, and was dating Joan Rivers' hairdresser. Tiberius and Keith had always had a very close relationship, and it made more sense for Tiberius to move back east. It was a win-win situation because this would allow each boy to get more focused attention. Keith could focus more attention on Tiberius, while David and I could do the same with Allard.

When Tiberius left to go live in New York, I asked David to consider couples counseling. David's response was that we were already engaged in family counseling. I explained that, first, it was hard to make any progress on that front without the boys' participation; and second, the focus of that therapy was on how to blend our family, not about our relationship with each other. I said family therapy would do little good if he and I didn't work on our relationship with each other. Inside myself, I had this feeling—which started that night when Keith called David from the Oakland airport, and David called me for advice—that I would never be very high on David's list of priority people. Even after all this time, I could never shake this feeling of being a fifth wheel in David's life, and that was no basis for a relationship.

David agreed that from the outset, our relationship was affected by a lot of situations that would have torn others apart far sooner. I began to list them: Keith's addiction; David suing for child custody; school behavioral assessments;

David's mother, Sheryl, almost dying; Keith's refusal to return the boys following a summer visit; Tiberius hanging out with gangsters and drug dealers and getting arrested; Allard becoming a father at sixteen; Allard losing a child at sixteen; Tiberius trying to kill me; caregiving for Abuela; infidelity; crystal meth addiction; David's father having a heart attack; three child protective services investigations; and a permanently unstable financial situation due to no child support. My point in listing these situation to David was to demonstrate to him that any two of the issues we'd experienced would break any "normal" couple apart; and yet, there we were having this conversation, despite it all. That in and of itself should have demonstrated to David just how dedicated I was to making our marriage work.

I gave David a ninety-day deadline with some conditions. For the next ninety days, we would make it a point to spend at least two days and two evenings together—evenings where we were not allowed to discuss children, family, Keith, or work—focusing on only each other. These evenings could be spent watching television, going to see a movie, attending a play, or having dinner with adult friends and couples. You know, the things most normal couples get to do. I took off my wedding ring and handed it to him, telling him that at the end of ninety days, he would either slip it back onto my finger or not.

On the evening of January 1, 2010—the ninety-first day—I found a white number ten business envelope in *mi abuelita*'s mailbox. It contained a gold band with a single diamond inset: my wedding ring. The following day, I contacted an attorney who was referred by the AIDS Legal Referral Panel, a nonprofit that links people living with HIV/AIDS to free or low-cost legal services in the Bay Area. On August 11 of that year, my marriage was officially dissolved. And just like that, my "until death us do part" died. Oh, I knew it had died long before that envelope was slipped into *mi abuelita*'s mailbox, but this made it final. Oddly, my thoughts weren't about my now ex-husband. They were about those two amazing young boys who had taught me quite a few things. In fact, I think I learned more from them than the other way around. I learned how resilient kids are; I learned how to truly put another's needs ahead of my own. I learned, quite to my surprise, how good a parent I could be, which in turn showed me that my parents weren't as bad as I thought. Some things they had done seemed to work; those that didn't, I tried not to repeat.

About three months later, *mi abuelita* passed away. So with her gone and my marriage over, I suffered an identity crisis of sorts. If I wasn't a husband, a grandson, a caregiver, a stepparent any longer, then what *was* I? I had no clue. I knew I needed to get far away from San Francisco and go someplace where I could lick my wounds and figure out just exactly what this new chapter of my life was going to look like . . . and that is exactly what I did.

Community Aftercare in Queer Leather Divorces

SASSAFRAS PATTERDALE

As teenagers, we fell brokenhearted fumbling into each other. We loved as hard as the streets our families threw us onto. We slept in piles, huddled in punk house living rooms and indie bookstores, while bands played at underground venues, in the back seats of cars on late-night drives to nowhere. We loved each other back into existence. We claimed and saved each other in ways that counselors and youth workers never could. As homeless queer youth, we knew we were all we had. Life was *show me yours and I'll show you mine*, trauma and dreams crashing together. We made promises we hoped we could keep to save each other, pressed bodies in hard hugs to seal our loyalty. I got a crash course on queer commitment from street kids and punk kids at seventeen when I came out, got kicked out, and started building my own family and worlds.

At twenty I met the person I would spend the next nineteen years married to, and more intensely in a 24/7 power dynamic with. They didn't come from the same queer worlds I did, and yet we fell into conversation in line for an after-Pride drag show. They said they were slumming it with a punk boi while on summer break from their private college. I was flagging a hunter green handkerchief in my right rear pocket: hanky code for boi seeking daddy. They said they wanted to take care of me. I fell in love. I gave him everything.

Imagine learning that everything you thought you had was a lie. Imagine trusting someone with your life. Imagine that they behaved honorably for almost two decades—until they didn't. Imagine coming home from a doctor's appointment only to discover your Daddy had been living a double life and planning to detonate your family and 24/7 total power exchange dynamic. Imagine they took half the money in your joint bank account without you knowing. Imagine learning your nineteen-year relationship was over via an email.

I had worried something was wrong, sensed the distance . . . but he told me everything was fine. Then when I came home one day, my cat was gone, my Daddy had been lying and had left, and my world, our home, the family I thought I had built, were all destroyed.

Divorce by its nature is devastating, but I believe that queer divorce is a particular sort of unmoored tragedy. As queer people, we fought to make our lives, our identities, and our bodies legitimate. We fought to have our relationships recognized and validated within systems designed to exclude us. I have never been so aggressively gendered as I was throughout my divorce process. This was especially funny given that I have been out as genderqueer for well over two decades. Before same-sex marriage was legal, my ex and I were married in a queer subversion of the system because as a genderqueer weirdo, I had changed my gender on my legal documents to male, and my ex (also trans) hadn't yet done so. When we were divorcing, I had spent the last several years playing with queer femininity, which meant I somehow became a "wife" and my ex the "husband." My ex and I had structured our life as a 24/7 total power exchange dynamic wherein I was the submissive, the boi to his Daddy. In our relationship, I was (until the very end) well cared for, but I had very little access to practical aspects of our life, such as the details of our finances. In the midst of divorce, I found myself needing to translate my queer life, body, and relationship structure to a legal system not designed for us.

I found and was saved by the leather community at the age of eighteen at the boots of leather queers who built me up, helped me see myself, and showed me the power inherent in submission. Submission doesn't mean you can't do something. It means you are choosing to give a part of yourself over, and you are leaning into (hopefully) well-earned trust. For me, being a leather person isn't just about who I'm sleeping with or what we do. Being a leather person is who I am in every interaction I have. I am alive because of community, so everything I have done in terms of art came from a place of service, of wanting to give back and repay some of what I was given. As a queer author, I have always understood myself and my work as existing in service to community. I can't fix things for everyone, but what I can do is make people feel a little less alone, create worlds on the page that mirror our queer lives. Everything I do, every book I write, and every workshop I teach is about being of service to community. For me, this is what it means to have good form as a person in the world.

My ex-partner and I lived in a 24/7 Daddy/boi power dynamic for over nineteen years, and we were legally married for sixteen of those years (our relationship predated the legalization of same-sex marriage). This dynamic dictated far more about our commitment than a marriage contract ever could. I consented to them caring for me. I trusted them to make major decisions for us. My ex-Daddy controlled where we lived, our financial decisions, what jobs I took, and what music I could listen to. They also controlled my gender presentation, whether I was allowed to cut my hair (I wasn't), what tattoos I got, and how I dressed. Now, I can unpack the ways their protocol overstretched what was reasonable or what I intended to consent to; and yet at the time, all I wanted was to be a good boi, even when, in the last two years, they started lying and sneaking around. I genuinely believed if I was good enough, well-behaved enough, they would stop acting weird and be the Daddy I loved, honored, and respected.

I used to think my relationship was perfect. My ex-partner and I once cowrote an advice column about queer/leather relationships. Friends regularly approached us for advice as the longest-lasting queer couple they knew. We were, I believed, genuinely happy for many years. "Compatible in life and leather" was how we described ourselves, and that was the glue that held us together, year in and year out. I had no idea that my partner wanted something different—not because I didn't ask, but because that truth was concealed from me. I followed the leather protocol; I did what I was told. I was a good boi. I taught about BDSM and how to have and navigate these kinds of ethical power exchange dynamics, and I expected those closest to me to have the same kind of ethics I did. For me, leather is not only how I want to structure my relationships and what I find erotically interesting; most importantly, it's a code of ethics, a way of engaging with the community. It's a standard that I hold myself to in terms of how I engage with people.

The night my ex-Daddy left, my dog and I wandered our house aimlessly. I didn't know if my ex was watching the security system. There was an ice storm outside, and there was nowhere I could go. I wandered from room to room trying to make sense of what had been there, what they had taken, and who I was going to be. I blasted '90s country, a genre of music I wasn't allowed to listen to for the majority of our relationship. I did not do my formerly required daily journal entry—something that had been nonnegotiable during our life together. At that moment I couldn't comprehend everything that was challenging, but I knew I needed to take ownership of my own life. Later, an old friend told me to be my own Daddy, and that became my immediate survival strategy. I needed to figure out how to wrestle my entire existence away from the memory of who I had submitted everything to for most of my adult life.

This divorce has been one of the biggest betrayals of my life, second only to being kicked out as a teenager for being queer. What was most devastating was the realization that I had given my submission to someone who I now know was unworthy and unwilling to ethically end what we had before pursuing a new life. Leather/BDSM relationships and community function because of complete trust and respect between everyone involved. Although people outside the community often don't realize this, the submissive partner is not weak, and submission is difficult. In my dynamic, I was required to express and verbalize any fear, any uncertainty, and I did. I didn't break rules. I did as I was told, and I was repeatedly assured that I had nothing to worry about. I was told the only thing I was doing wrong was doubting and questioning whether something was wrong. For nearly twenty years I had been trained to trust their perspective over my own. I wanted to be a good boi, so I listened. Learning that I had been lied to was far more devastating than any other typical divorce betrayal, like having an affair.

"You have to tell your attorney about your power dynamic," one of my closest friends told me the night after my partner left. I'd written and taught about leather relationship dynamics for years; and yet, early in the divorce, I hadn't realized how our dynamic could be weaponized against me. I hadn't understood how that power dynamic influenced the (lack of) power I held in our relationship, which—much to my own frustration—left me extremely vulnerable in these early divorce negotiations. Because of the specifics of our power dynamic, I only had vague ideas about our finances, I wasn't allowed more detailed information for years, and ultimately I did what I had been trained in leather to do: I trusted my Dom, because until that point they hadn't shown me anything to make me question that. The detonation of my relationship threw me into an immediate crisis. I had been systematically isolated from the community, and I didn't even have control over the security system in my home. When we were together, these things felt like negotiated containment, and the moment they left, it felt like bondage I couldn't break free from. I was thrown into an instant, uncontained sub drop (*sub drop* is a community term that references the emotional, mental, physical, and spiritual crash or vulnerability that often happens after a BDSM scene or upon the dissolution of a BDSM power dynamic).

My divorce would have been so much worse if I hadn't notified my attorney right away about what my life had actually looked like and the way our total power exchange dynamic permeated every aspect of my life. During this process, I was lucky to be getting queer divorced in a liberal city, in a queer-affirming state where I was able to hire a leather-competent attorney who was herself queer, and where the former judge who served as a mediator for our divorce was culturally competent and prepared to understand the complications of a queer divorce. I had changed my name early in our relationship as part of our leather/power exchange dynamic before same-sex marriage was even legal. As part of the divorce process, I took my last name back, returning to the one I had chosen for myself as a punk zine writer publishing my truth and building my queer life for the first time without ties to biological family.

Nobody gets married thinking they are going to get divorced. Similarly, nobody enters a 24/7 power exchange dynamic and follows the attendant intense daily protocol for over nineteen years expecting that one day they will come home to find out their life as they knew it is over. I was not an inexperienced submissive. I trusted the dynamic. I trusted the protocol. I took pride in being a total power exchange leather boi. Coming home from a doctor's appointment to an email saying my marriage was ending—confirming my fears that they had been deliberately dishonest with me—shattered my world.

When my ex-Daddy left, each day felt like waking up in a nightmare. Everything was surreal. Nothing about my world made sense. People fall out of love, people break up, but to walk away without an explanation and sending an email saying you're building a new life involving someone else felt like such a cishet thing to do. It was hard to map that story onto my extremely queer life. As a full-time artist, I threw myself into creating and surviving. Fortunately, my queer family, well-established and also newly created, stepped into my life in ways I didn't expect. They circled around me and made sure I had someone to talk to daily, made new holiday traditions with me, let me be of service to our family, and literally held me as my very ugly queer/leather divorce fought its way into legitimacy through the cishet legal system.

My queer and leather family loved me when I was sure nobody ever could again. They helped me believe I hadn't deserved the way I had been treated. They helped me love myself back onto my feet and believe I could start over at forty. As my queer/leather family held me physically and energetically through starting over, I realized that what they were doing was giving me the leather aftercare that I needed and hadn't received. In BDSM/leather culture, when a scene ends, the standard practice is for the scene participants to transition directly into aftercare, which involves the participants taking time together to decompress and come down from the heightened energy of the scene. Aftercare is essentially an embodiment of processing the emotional impact of the experience so the participants can recenter and return to self. Aftercare helps everyone involved in the scene come back to who they were before play, to steady themselves so they are ready to reengage with the world. At this point my closest queer family and I began using the phrase "community aftercare" to talk about what it was like to hold me through this process. Community aftercare isn't just the times I fall apart crying on my best friends' kitchen floor while petting their cats. Community aftercare is about showing up for the good days as well as the hard ones.

I was doing everything I could to hold myself together, but we are not made to exist alone. My chosen queer/leather family near and far provided the practical community aftercare my ex-Daddy decided not to provide. They helped me remember who I am, who I was before this relationship, and who I wanted to be after it.

The minute I posted online that my relationship had ended, my world opened. My best author friends flooded my text messages and inboxes, and friends and acquaintances showed up. Community aftercare isn't just about checking in; it's about being an unwavering presence. Community aftercare is sending memes, it's laughing so hard you choke on your bubble tea, it's postcards and care packages in my mailbox, reminding me people are standing with me. Even before my ex left, I was terrified I was washed up as an author/artist. This tragedy has shown me how wrong I was. Community aftercare is people on multiple continents I know I can text any time, day or night, who will show up. Community aftercare is a commitment to a shared existence. Community aftercare means nobody gets left behind. Community aftercare is a recognition of how hard you fought to get where you are, and that it's okay to rest, to trust that other people will take care of you. I'm a submissive, but that doesn't mean I'm not capable. I don't like asking for help. Still, community aftercare in the immediate aftermath of my divorce meant surrounding myself with people who understood what I sacrificed and who stood behind me as I told my story and rebuilt a life that was more queerly authentic than the box I had been stuck in.

"Why are people being so nice to me?" I've asked repeatedly. When my ex-Daddy left, I thought I was unlovable. Surely, if the person who had loved me for two decades was walking out of my life to get a divorce, then I was unworthy of love, care, and respect. Part of my journey has been unlearning those messages. It is accepting that those closest to me are right when they say my whole queer life until this point has been about showing up, about serving the community. It has been an opportunity for me to allow the community I have served to show up and hold me. I'm told I've "earned it," and while I'm not sure I fully believe that, I do feel deeply the ways in which my community near and far has woven a web of support that holds me, even on my hardest days.

One of the biggest surprises of my divorce has been the unexpected joy of bringing me closer to my queer culture. Beyond the practical matters of whether I could keep living in my home, how bills would get paid, and ensuring I would have custody of my dog, one of the big questions I had to grapple with was what it meant to me to be part of leather culture as a single person. I had spent nineteen years collared to someone, my community identity tied to that relationship, a relationship that looked like the Disneyland of leather dynamics. Magic and perfection was an image I put a lot of work into maintaining, not because I was trying to portray us as something we weren't, but because it's truly what I believed we were, and "accurately" portraying that was an act of service.

I was scared and embarrassed when one cruel email shattered my world. However, much to my amazement, the leather community caught me, steadied me in my boots, and emotionally helped me start over building my own life. I'll always be a leather boi at my core. As my divorce was finalized, I also for a short period of time made the decision to collar myself—a sign for myself and others that I am in community but that I am also a free agent and I belong to myself. I will never be the leather boi I was before my life was detonated. When my divorce first began, I said never again could I submit. I worried that leather was dead to me, and then who would I be? This had been my community home since I was eighteen. I love the ritual and the joy of power play in S/M. I believe this is part of my queer cultural legacy and what is home for me, and it can't be taken away. I believe that in many ways how this divorce was handled could have destroyed me; but like so many times in my life as a queer person, a genderqueer person, I was underestimated. I found and was saved by queer community every time my world fell apart.

There is an intimacy that develops among queer folks who have shared traumas and experiences. We can hold each other's fears and joys. We lift each other up. I'll let you see my soft and wounded places, and you won't hide yours. Together we will build new dreams. Together in queer magic, we will create something new out of loss and shattered plans. At the time of writing, my divorce is still fresh. It's too early to know exactly what my new life will look like, but I know I feel safe and happy and grounded for the first time in a long time. I feel like myself again. I also know that these queer and leather families I've forged are the only glue I need or want to hold together this new queer life I'm building. I am not the same leather boi I once was. Much to my surprise, I've discovered I'm a stronger and better boi than I ever was. Queer divorce might have shattered the life I thought I had, but it has also freed me.

Forever Family

CHRIS E. VARGAS

Greg and I were never technically married. We met in 2007, before same-sex marriage was legal. At the time, we were immersed in anti-assimilationist, Gay Shame, and feminist-of-color-informed critiques of same-sex marriage that were circulating in the mid-aughts in queer hotbeds like the Bay Area, where we both lived. These critiques emerged, or rather reemerged, in response to the intense fervor surrounding the massive, well-funded, national Right to Marry movement, with its homonormative aspirations toward normalcy and its failure—or refusal—to critically examine the real promises of marriage. The institution, created to make transfers of wealth among the owning class more seamless, also conferred hundreds of rights upon couples, including health care, hospital visits, citizenship, and tax breaks. But why were so many of these fundamental protections only afforded to married people? And what about the unhoused, the undocumented, the ill—the most vulnerable members of our communities? As a community, we should have been demanding more, and the refusal to participate in the institution was a way to put these politics into practice. These politics shaped both us as well as the broader queer community we were part of. Greg and I even made collaborative, creative artwork inspired by these very conversations within LGBTQ communities. But I'm getting ahead of myself.

We came together "against all odds"—or so it seemed, like many relationship narratives. On paper, we appeared very different. Him: cis and white. Me: trans and of mixed ethnicity—Chicano and European white. Stylistically, I signaled more "radically queer," while he looked like a normy gay—"a Castro gay," as my ex before Greg insultingly referred to him. The trans thing seemed the most difficult for people to grasp. Even within our very queer and trans circle, we knew only one other mixed-gender (cis and trans) gay couple. We had some hurdles to surmount, but in reality, we weren't so different.

We were only six months apart in age, and we both grew up in California—me in Los Angeles's San Fernando Valley, and him in the Central Valley town of Modesto. We both came of age at a particular moment in the '90s, part of Generation "Catalano," "Oregon Trail," or "Xennials," as we're often referred to—referencing, respectively, a character from the quintessential '90s TV show *My So-Called Life*, the early computer-based text adventure game *Oregon Trail*, and the generational cusp between Gen X and Millennials. The defining trait of this microgeneration is that we were the last to experience our tender, awkward middle and high school years without the scary internet and cruel social media. Because of this, Greg and I had nearly identical cultural references: We grew up on the same raucous and ridiculous daytime TV talk shows and infomercials, and we both remembered smoking sections in restaurants—and even in churches. The latter was Greg's memory, one he always questioned the validity of, because he remembers it also being the childcare section, where smoking moms bounced squalling babies behind soundproof glass.

I began my creative life as a filmmaker and video artist, while he was (and still is) a film scholar. He was my TA, the discussion section facilitator, for a bad film theory class I took at UC Santa Cruz, where I had transferred to from community college to complete my undergrad degree. That's how we met. I was a later-in-life transfer student, while he had gone through school on a more traditional timeline. That's when I first set my sights on him—a crush I nurtured throughout the rest of the academic year and through the end of a previous relationship.

It was a sweet, magical coming together: early dates with weak margaritas at Puerto Alegre in the Mission, homemade risotto at a house-sit near Lake Merritt, and finally, a romantic hike on December 13, 2007, at Redwood Regional Park in the Berkeley Hills—one that ended back at my place in north Oakland.

This date, our anniversary, was also the anniversary of my top surgery, which I had undergone exactly two years prior.

Within the first month of being together, we hatched and started production on an early YouTube web series that played with the seemingly pronounced differences between us, framing them within an "odd couple"-style sitcom format. It was a well-worn trope, but we had fun subverting it, laughing at the dissonance—the idea that we were performing characters far more different than we actually were. We made the first few videos quickly, and the project had a few viral moments, particularly when we weighed in on the Obama/McCain election. The project brought us to the MIX FEST queer experimental film festival in New York City and to the Tate Modern, where our videos screened as part of a retrospective for the iconic experimental filmmaker Barbara Hammer. This was a major highlight for us, as Greg had written about Hammer's work. We remained in touch with Barbara and her partner, Florrie Burke, who became our queer relationship role models.

From 2008 to 2013 we worked on the web series *Falling in Love . . . with Chris and Greg*, making ten episodes in total. Our work was deeply inspired by and intertwined with the issues we were navigating in our personal lives. We tackled topics like open relationships (in theory, not practice); body issues; sloppy Bay Area queer aesthetics and artists' refusals to move away from that aesthetic toward professionalization; same-sex marriage; and academic exploitation, particularly inspired by Greg's postdoctoral adjunct teaching. The latter was what eventually edged us out of the Bay Area. After he finished his dissertation in 2009, Greg began the exploitative adjunct teaching hustle—eventually teaching at three different universities simultaneously—while also writing his first book and searching for a tenure-track job, which is a full-time job in and of itself. After my two-year MFA at UC Berkeley, I was hustling too: adjuncting, though on a relatively smaller scale, at two nearby universities.

In 2012, it occurred to us that I could get on his university health plan and benefit from dental coverage as long as we were registered as "domestic partners." As part of my own hustle, I had been using a friend's San Francisco address to access trans-competent health care in the city. The low-cost queer clinic had been good to me, but my worsening teeth issues were proving too complex for the cheap dental school clinic in the area. Greg had moved in with my roommate and me about a year or so into our relationship, so the domestic part wasn't untrue. We printed forms from the internet and had them notarized at the local, run-down, beater car rental/notary public near our apartment in Oakland.

Rent-A-Relic had a cute plywood dinosaur sign perched over an office trailer that looked like it had been plunked down onto an empty parking lot on Telegraph Avenue. A white European backpacker who was dropping off a car agreed to take our picture under the dinosaur, and that became the closest thing we ever had to a wedding photo. I always thought it was pretty charming—akin to a Vegas wedding at a kitschy chapel—which actually rhymed with a scene from one of our videos where we tackled the issue of same-sex marriage and the radical queer critiques of it. Our characters in the episode "Road Trip! TV Special" found themselves at the altar with conflicting motivations for the protest gesture. But the real Chris and Greg were at Rent-A-Relic for practical purposes. It was a given that we loved each other.

A year later, in 2013, we left the Bay Area in pursuit of better academic job prospects elsewhere. *Falling in Love . . . with Chris and Greg* came to a close. We hadn't been making the videos at the speed we had in the beginning, and we couldn't surmount the tensions about the division of labor. And we also got busy with other projects and life. The last episode we made was a Golden Girls–style flashback clip reel of our favorite moments in the series, titled "Cheesecake and Memories."

In 2014, after a brief nine-month stopover in Hamilton, New York, where Greg did a stint at the small, elite liberal arts college there, we landed on our feet in Bellingham, Washington. We both had tenure-track teaching jobs—a dream for many academic couples. I continued making work, but we both detoured from video as our primary medium. We were still deeply involved in, and in conversation with, each other's respective practices. I had begun what would become a decade-long project, the Museum of Trans Hirstory & Art, and Greg began writing short and long-form fiction. We always wondered why we could never collaborate as easily again. It was one of those recurring conversations—a puzzle we returned to over and over. It was almost as if the heyday of our relationship was behind us, and we were continuously trying to find our way back. Or at least that's how it could be narrated after the fact. Another way to narrate it: We became adults. We got steady jobs, good health care (by US standards), and 401(k)s. We both got tenure. We bought a house. We traveled a lot. And the focus and pace of our own individual creative projects changed.

Another conversation we returned to over and over was marriage. In 2015, three years after the notary at Rent-A-Relic witnessed our domestic partnership, same-sex couples across the country could legally marry. The urgency of that earlier radical queer critique seemed to fade into the background as we saw many of our friends getting married—some for practical reasons like adoption or health care, and others in ways that suited their particular preferences, like beautiful, witchy ceremonies in the woods where blades of grass served as rings. But we could never reach a place of agreement about the topic. Or rather, Greg was never satisfied with the outcomes of this conversation.

This is how it went. Greg would bring up the topic of marriage. I would ask, "Why? What's the point?" We both had jobs and health care, we owned a house with both our names on the title, and we had already been together for so many years. He would point to the ritualistic significance, comparing it to how we pulled tarot cards at the start of every new year or celebrated the winter and summer solstices. I could see his perspective. I'd acquiesce. But then we'd talk out the shape of this ritualistic gathering and reach the question that brought the discussion to a halt: Would we invite our families? Though we both had functional relationships with our families, it seemed too difficult to imagine bringing them all together with our queer friends, merging all the different parts of our lives. It felt too awkward, too complicated, and expensive.

Despite our many similarities and shared cultural touchstones, we had very different parental relationship models. I grew up with a young, single mom who had many partners over the years. She had me when she was barely twenty years old, and though she was clearly my parent, I also watched her grow up. I was aware that she was young—especially in relation to my friends' parents. Her various boyfriends made sense to me as companions for the particular developmental moments in her life. Her life modeled something for me that made sense: You're with someone for as long as it works, for as long as it makes sense for who you are at that moment. People grow, needs change, and paths more often than not will likely diverge. I understood this in relation to gender and age, too. I'd seen how my needs and desires changed as I grew up and transitioned. The model my mom unknowingly gave me aligned really well with my queer conception and approach to relationships, and I am so thankful to her.

Greg's parents, on the other hand, are still together to this day. They are older, closer to my grandparents' age. They persevered through a lot of difficult moments, much like I saw my grandparents do. But to me, this always felt needless. Why stay together when you could simply move on to the next right fit? I don't think Greg saw it that way.

Over a decade in, no one was more surprised than I that I had been in a relationship that could have easily lasted forever. Greg and I got along so well. We shared a brain. If I believed in the idea of a single soulmate, it would be him. His cisness in the beginning validated my identity as a gay man. He was never straight, so being with him never complicated my own identity. He was a gay-gay through and through. He liked Broadway and Patti LuPone, and he'd worshipped a series of divas as a kid—Madonna, Marilyn Monroe, Paula Abdul. I still think he's the smartest, funniest person I've ever met.

But in 2019, almost twelve years into our relationship, a crack began to appear.

It was early in that year when Greg went to a film conference and reunited with a bunch of middle-aged colleagues and friends. He discovered that many people who had been in long-term relationships were opening them up. At first I was completely averse to the idea; but nevertheless, it planted a seed. For months, that seed germinated; then, something sprouted. I went out of town to a trans male sleepaway camp. My friend, a cofounder of this visionary camp where "men of trans experience" get to relive, for the first time, a summer camp boyhood, had invited me to attend. Funnily enough, while at the camp I facilitated a conversation about relationships. The conversation went well enough, but I realized that there were so many concerns with trans people in relationships that I didn't relate to, such as disclosing, or changing genders in partnerships, thereby altering people's conception of themselves and their partners' sexual identities. There were so many different ways that one's transness impacted their relationships, but having been in such a long-term thing, these ceased being an issue for me.

It was there that I met someone. For the first time in over a decade, I felt a deep attraction to someone that couldn't be ignored. He was also trans, of course. He was Chicano—tall, bearded, so handsome. The attraction was overwhelming. My brain was so flooded with chemicals that I couldn't sleep. I found reasons to be in his orbit and stayed up late to hang out with him, but nothing happened between us there. Even so, I couldn't put him out of my mind. The fact that he was trans and Chicano was significant. I desired the affirmation that both of these shared identities could provide. My ethnicity needed to be affirmed, or I desired to relate to a nonwhite person intimately.

When I returned, high on this new crush, I talked with Greg more seriously about opening our relationship up. The rest of the year saw a slow processing and unfolding of this arrangement. I stayed in touch with summer camp guy. Months later, I confessed my crush to him; months after that, we hung out, and he confessed his attraction to me. Then, at the end of the year, we had our first official date. I had fallen in deep.

Then 2020 happened. During the global pandemic, Greg and I continued to navigate an open relationship. It was so painful. It became clear that this affair was opening something in me that I needed to explore; not with this person necessarily, though my attraction to him was hard to ignore, but something beyond. In fact, it was always clear it wasn't about him, even though I did fall in love with him. To pursue this affair, I took pandemic risks I shouldn't have, like taking plane rides for weekend visits when no one else was flying. Luckily, there were no dire consequences or infections. The draw was so strong. I had reached a midlife fork in the road: I could stay on my current path of stability and commitment to a life full of love I had built with Greg, or I could move toward an embodied life of experiences, adventure, and the unknown. I knew that these two paths couldn't coexist. Polyamory was revealing itself to be unworkable for Greg and me. Greg did, in fact, want something more conventional, and while I wasn't sure polyamory was right for me, I knew I needed to do some exploring.

Bellingham, the job, homeownership, being identified only as part of a couple, not as an individual—it all began to feel so uncomfortable. The fact that the town and the university I taught at were majority white was not lost on me. Being mixed had prepared me to navigate such situations, but I felt wholly illegible in this place, in this job. I had tried to make it work for so long. It was finally time to make a leap out of this place, out of this job, out of this life. I had to do it alone. I needed to be back in LA. In my addled state, it felt riskier to do it with another person; I don't know why. Perhaps if I was going to try and fail, it had to be on my own. Also, I wanted to know who I was as an individual, not as part of a unit. It had been so long.

Greg and I officially broke up in August 2020.

The best thing we did during the breakup was to start seeing an amazing couples counselor over Zoom who helped us navigate the hard feelings and commit to being "forever family." And we remained close for so many years after our official breakup. The breakup was the prolonged discomfort of a slow tearing off of a Band-Aid. Though I was living off and on in LA, we didn't fully move out of our house in Bellingham until a year after our official break, in the summer of 2021, when we both started our simultaneous nine-month sabbaticals. Even after that, we talked nearly every day and joined each other on platonic trips in foreign countries. The breakup grief unfolded in stages. One big stage of grief hit when I was in Berlin in the summer of 2022, delirious with jet lag, wanting to reach out—but Greg was with his new boyfriend in Argentina. Another wave came in fall 2022, when my new boyfriend came to Bellingham to help me drive a truckload of my stuff down to LA. Having him there in my old town, having these worlds collide, was so disorienting. Another big wave hit when, after years of remote teaching, I returned to Bellingham to teach in person for the last time in spring 2024. By then, Greg was deep into his new relationship, setting up what I experienced as really harsh boundaries. Then there was the finality of quitting the job in the summer of 2024—one of the jobs we had gotten together. This was also the same summer Greg announced he was engaged to be married.

The process of untangling our thirteen years together continues to this day. While I was writing the essay for this book, Greg began looking more deeply into buying me out of the house we still co-owned, along with starting to navigate the incredibly unwieldy process of the ninety-day fiancé visa his future husband would need in order to come to the US. Greg learned two surprising and contradictory things. First, it might not be so easy to simply borrow money and buy me out of the house while maintaining the low interest rate we had secured in 2016. Greg would have to reapply for a loan and incur a $10,000 "excising" fee to get my name off the title. And second, which might actually solve the first issue, the domestic partner certificate we had notarized at the Rent-a-Relic in Oakland back in 2012 was still valid and would need to be dissolved so there weren't any snags on his path to marrying his new fiancé. When same-sex marriage became legal, we assumed that domestic partnerships were rendered meaningless. In fact, back in 2015, I remember us jokingly searching the internet to make sure our domestic partnership hadn't been rolled over into a same-sex marriage. It became obvious that we hadn't done too much digging back then, because recently Greg found out our domestic partnership might still be valid, and he quickly assigned his immigration lawyer the task of dissolving it.

We had never been married, but now we have to get gay divorced. So humiliating.

A lot of people say it, and now I understand. It's so easy to get married and so hard to get divorced—emotionally, financially, and administratively. But again, we were never married in the true legal sense. We were the sad, earlier gay version of married: domestic partnered. Or "DP'd," as Greg would say. However, the paperwork that our lawyer got us to fill out made it seem as if we had indeed been married. We had to formalize all the ways we had already privately and easily negotiated the separation of "our" assets, including the future buying out of our house. It wasn't hard, but implied in the minutiae was the tension we were supposed to feel between us because of the uncoupling—and the legal guardrails it was providing to us should the tides of emotion turn.

It felt strange. Very *Kramer vs. Kramer*, a movie I've never seen but feel like I understand the gist of. It was all very impersonal, sure; but mostly it was a weird fit, the way the thought of marriage always seemed to be. I felt like I was fitting myself into an institution that wasn't built to accommodate me—much like being trans and navigating administrative and health care systems. Also, the relationship between Greg and me was special. I suppose, in some ways, I thought that the institution could never truly recognize that, and I didn't care to make the institution understand how unique the relationship was.

I think this might've been a bigger difference between us than I knew: Greg's adeptness in navigating these systems, and perhaps a sense or hope that he could gain all the benefits promised therein, and my ever-existing distrust, cynicism, and desire to find meaning in other ways. I've navigated these systems with varying degrees of honesty, so perhaps this bred a deep distrust in these systems' ability to truly see me. On the other hand, Greg is really good at it, as I watch him navigate his and his new partner's immigration process. Maybe that's actually the difference: this comes easier for him, as a cis white guy, the same way he is "naturally" good at standardized tests.

As I write this, just after Trump's second inauguration, we are in the midst of an even bigger than imagined backlash against trans existence and undocumented people in the US—the former targeting trans people's very existence, access to appropriate IDs, and medical care. As many radical trans activists have pointed out, we never need to look to the government to legitimize our identities (and relationships). But there are so many ways we have to interact with systems; and wanting to do it with a sense of dignity, safety, and one's full true self is noble. But not always possible.

I still miss Greg all the time. We did life really well together. Even navigating this "divorce" process has been so easy with him. It's strange to walk away from something that wasn't bad or embroiled in misery and conflict. My love and respect for him is so deep that I always want him to be happy. I will always be grateful for the thirteen years we spent together and for the person I am as a result of sharing those important early and middle adult years. We became adults together. Now I look forward to watching him continue to develop as a person, writer, thinker, and I'll always be supporting him and cheering him on. From afar. As Greg and I rebuild our lives separately, my own network of friends and community continues to broaden. Now more than ever, I see that the legitimacy we seek—for our relationships, identities, and potential for liberation—has always existed within the sweet queer and trans communities we build for ourselves. I'm realizing more clearly than ever that it has always been about the communities and chosen families we create. And I trust deeply that Greg and I will always consider each other "forever family."

The Farmer and the Snake (农夫与蛇 Nóng fū yǔ shé)

SHAO FU

Author's note: Suggested music accompaniment for this essay: "The Moon Got in My Eyes" by Mildred Bailey.

My mind plays the story on repeat every day: a sunlit living room with handsome wooden furniture. A picture on the fireplace mantel shows a grinning young woman with long black hair and a tall man. *Click!* A second framed photo depicts their engagement—a gender-swapping surprise in which the woman proposes while dressed in a black tulle skirt, surrounded by loved ones under an archway of flowers. *Click!* A series of photos follows, capturing not one but three weddings—a testament to their grand love and commitment to each other.

The first wedding, atop a mountain at sunset, is bathed in golden leaves. The second wedding takes place in a cozy cabin with friends. The same bride looks ethereal in a fitted dress and cascading burgundy hair, while the groom wears a dapper suit. The final wedding photo shows the couple laughing joyfully with family, their cheeks flushed after reading their vows. *Click!* One memory after another, the living room reflects a happy home, with a camera roll full of cherished moments. It feels good.

The story moves forward. The couple prepares for a night out. The woman takes a needle and injects testosterone into the man while he stands shirtless in front of the bathroom mirror. She looks at his newly healed chest scars and confirms out loud that she too wants to get top surgery and start taking testosterone. They embrace, but he notices her worried face. "My darling," he says, "our bodies will change regardless! How we were when we first met will be vastly different with age, and we're going to look very old, because I'm going to love you for forever. I love you not for your appearance, but for who you are on the inside," he promises her. *Click!*

Now the couple stands in their living room. They are flabbergasted. "Seven million dollars?" the man says. "I can't believe it . . ." He clutches his wife's hands excitedly and stares deeply into her eyes. "This will literally change our life." She nods in disbelief. They quietly kiss. *Click!*

At last, there's a long, dark alley. The nighttime air is crisp, and everything echoes off the cobblestones. The woman holds the man's hand firmly, ready to protect him with her life. Suddenly a rustling sound reveals a stranger in the shadows. The stranger points a gun at the couple. *Click!*

When the woman opens her eyes a moment later, she realizes her husband's hands are gripping her by the arms. He had shoved her directly in front of him. The woman stares at the bullet wound in her chest with confusion. The man lets go, and the woman's knees hit the ground as she collapses. At first, the husband appears distant and cold as he stands over her, staring at her, but then his face twists into a look of disgust. He steps over her body and disappears into the night.

The story's ending hits hard every time. I always try to resist it, convinced my love was "different." I thought we were the exception. Aren't trans people synonymous with unicorns, rainbows, and fairytales? Each tender memory only deepens my confusion. When people ask how I have been since the divorce, this fantasy comes to mind, because basic words to describe feelings aren't enough to convey the betrayal and heartbreak.

To speak vulnerably, I feel a deep shame at having been deceived and abandoned by my spouse, because my family warned me. In the Chinese fable "The Farmer and the Snake" ("Nóng fū yǔ shé"), a kind farmer saves a snake, only to be bitten by it. The practical lesson is that compassion should be tempered with wisdom, since everyone you help won't behave honestly. I heard my parents, aunties, and grandparents echo these warnings on repeat with each person I fell in love with, so I eventually drowned their voices out.

How much longer will my heart keep bleeding? I trusted the long, sincere-sounding text messages and the deep eye contact. I believed the piles of dramatic love letters from him. Friends witnessed his gratuitous public displays of affection toward me. I had so many tangible artifacts of proof that, contrary to what my ancestors said, this love is real! He would protect and adore me because his words are real! There are actually good people out there whose words can be trusted . . .

The Chinese tale is summarized by the saying: "Kindness to the wicked is cruelty to oneself." My husband had said all the "right" things, yet here I am, metaphorically lying on the ground with a bullet in my heart. Life taught me I'd die for him. It also taught me he wouldn't do the same.

You can be a good person and still find yourself divorced. You can be in the coveted T4T relationship and still be divorced. You can be a great spouse and still end up divorced. You can be cautious, or not, and still get divorced. I learned that part of living a life without regret means following your heart, regardless of the outcome. Fables, sage advice, metaphors, and lore cannot save you from a tragic end. With that said, you also don't die from a broken heart.

Click! Time has passed. Now when I imagine that fantastical story of myself lying on the cobblestones with a bleeding heart, that is not the ending. Instead, I see the transitioned version of myself climbing over rocks and ruins, dirtied but determined, decades later. The betrayal is a lesson learned in the past. The scarred heart still beats. I hold my backpack of essentials tight while I survey the wilderness that stretches out beyond. I do not know where I am traveling to, and that is okay.

A Marriage of Masking

RAE-MOSES EPSTEIN

"I don't love you the way a wife should love her husband."

The funny thing is, I didn't know I was transgender when my husband came out of the shower and joked that I could *Forgetting Sarah Marshall* him. I just told him to get dressed, led him down to the kitchen table in the San Diego rental we had just moved into from New Jersey, and that's what popped out of my mouth.

Even now, I can understand why people mistook me for a girl my entire life. The first shrine I built was to my mother's wedding portrait. From the age of two onward, I'd sit in her bedroom and gaze upon the 1980s-style puffed sleeves on her dress, her gleaming smile, and the cascades of white lilies in her bouquet. My mother as a bride seemed like a queen. I dreamed of having my own day as a white-gowned monarch.

That came with a price, in the end. Those lilies, her favorite flower, also made an appearance at my wedding, upon her insistence. I threw desperate, pleading looks to the florist, because that was not the only time my special day became my mother's second chance at her own wedding to my father. The florist kindly brokered a compromise and had the lilies woven into the chuppah.

I'll always remember that indignity, as well as the cover-up makeup that easily sweated off of my tattoos and permanently stained my own beautiful dress. I did not want to cover up my body art; my parents thought the tattoos "ruined" my look as a bride. However, like with my first-choice tiara, my husband cautioned that refusing the cover-up would lead to a fight with my mother. So I acquiesced.

All in all, it turned out to be a beautiful day. I did want, and was overall happy, to become a bride.

However, did I want to be a wife?

Well . . . I'd never thought that far ahead.

My relationship with my ex-husband started off like a romantic comedy. We met when he was nineteen and a journalism major living in San Diego, and I was twenty-two, living in New York City and working my first copywriter job. Facebook linked us in a group of comic book journalists. I didn't like him that much at first, writing him off as some dumb, immature kid. But eventually he won me over. Once he mailed me a box of comics I'd wanted and left a romance comic at the top. My friend smirked at me knowingly as my face turned bright red upon opening the box.

I identified as bisexual, and proudly so. Much of my journalism work focused on platforming queer comic books and their creators. So when we got together years later, my ex in one of his many forms of support talked to me about how we were a queer couple even if he was a cishet man. We introduced each other as "partners" to others as we attended queer-heavy comics conventions. I would pick up the provided pronoun badges—she/her, of course—and exclaim, "Oh! I love these. It makes *me* feel safer knowing they're trying to help *others* feel safer, you know?" and he would look at me quizzically.

At home in New Jersey—in close proximity to my always-critical parents, and enshrouded in a world of cisheterosexual, suburban white normalcy—we called each other "boyfriend" and "girlfriend." My autistic husband had a superhero-level ability to mask. I once told him, to his horror, that he came off to strangers as an "enterprising young man." He didn't actually like people or want to interact with them, but I found protection while under his umbrella of fake neurotypicality. He taught me to censor myself so I wouldn't tell my parents too much, gave me good excuses to leave their house early after dinner, and helped rebuild my self-image after it was still inevitably ripped into again and again.

We got along so well that we did not fight once while in the COVID-19 pandemic lockdown. Within the first few days of that once-in-a-lifetime event, we got engaged, and the following year and a half paved the way toward our future divorce. As a former dabbler in witchcraft and a polytheist who had yet to explore my interest, I used my newfound free time to learn to read tarot and discover new depths of the occult. My first shrines since my mother's wedding portrait quickly arose and populated our small apartment.

This was much to my ex's consternation. He was a staunch materialist atheist—although you wouldn't know that from the comics he put out during our relationship, on Jewish golems and the Greek god Dionysus—and my religious fervor made him uncomfortable. Although he tried to be supportive, including when I started reading tarot professionally at a small metaphysical store in our town, he couldn't hide his dislike for all of it. *Especially* when I began to study astrology. "You promised me that was the one thing you wouldn't do!" he said.

Somehow, we overlooked this massive divergence in values and became "husband" and "wife." I needed to emotionally survive my circumstances, and he enjoyed completing a bachelor's degree while being mostly financially supported. In New Jersey, our relationship made perfect sense.

California must have laughed when it first saw us.

A month and a half. That's how long our marriage lasted in San Diego.

Once my body realized that I was, in fact, not on vacation and it was not going home to New Jersey, it freaked out. I spent the very beginning of my time in my new home region having panic attacks as soon as night fell. A year prior, the same primal fear had fallen upon me as I burned out from wedding planning and saw a spider cricket in our basement. *Share your feelings via noise*, said the omen. So I screamed and sobbed then. And I screamed and sobbed again.

It dawned on me, quite horribly, that I had spent my entire life in service of my parents' image of what I should be. I had attended the college they wanted me to attend, only forty minutes away from them. I immediately got a job in the same industry as my father upon graduation, because he arranged an interview at a company I ultimately hated, in a role I could not excel in. When

I failed at the path my parents squeezed me into, I was forced to move back to New Jersey, where my ex mercifully joined me.

Many would probably sneer at me, insisting that I was an adult, a privileged one at that, and I had "choices." But I was so emotionally cauterized from who I was as a person that I did not know that I had a second gender that was male for most of my life. How could I have made different choices with that kind of steerage?

At any rate, in San Diego I no longer had my lifelong scaffolding, and for the first time I could see the truth. There was no "one way" to do anything. No particular goals, no particular job, no particular way to *be.*

This left the question: Who was me?

I had to clear the rest of the rubble and rebuild. My marriage was naturally the first thing to go, given that my husband and I had nothing in common at that point but our dogs. The initial effort to get my ex to leave was rough. However, during our two-hour closure call that happened about six months after he moved out of San Diego, he admitted, "Thank you for pulling the trigger. I never would have. But our marriage was never going to last."

One other nice thing about California is that it has several kinds of "dissolutions," which is a very polite word for divorce. Among them is a "summary dissolution." All my ex and I had to do was live in the state for six months. We wrote up a document explaining how we were going to split our insignificant shared property, which we submitted to the courthouse along with the other signed papers. I gave him a small bit of one-time alimony, he took one dog, and I kept the one I have had since college. He always had trans friends, so now I'm just one more.

We had a wonderful wedding with weather so many would die for, delicious lobster rolls, and a fall color scheme. We had an equally nice divorce.

I often think of the meme showing two identical men sitting on opposite sides of a train car. One looks miserably at a wall. The other smiles with bright hope as he watches a beautiful view pass by outside the window. In my thoughts, they always say the same thing as each other, with different outlooks:

I will never be a bride again. I will never be a bride again.

I am currently in my first serious relationship since my marriage ended. I met my girlfriend on an occult Discord server she moderated, in the astrology channel where we learned together the meanings of our strangely complementary natal charts. She worships the same deities as I do, has experimented with much of the same magic, and practices her own forms of divination. My regular psychic reader told me a long time ago that she is one of my soulmates. Even if she wasn't, she is the most gorgeous woman in existence, highlighted by the fact that she is just as trans as I am.

I would love to be her husband someday.

If Not Her

PAISLEY CORNELL

If not her, then who?

That's what comes to mind when I considered proposing to Sarah, now my ex-wife. Not exactly the enthusiastic declaration of love that movies and TV have conditioned us to expect for a decision as monumental as marriage (see the movie *The Notebook* for dramatic contrast). But unlike Ryan Gosling and Rachel McAdams' characters, nothing in my life ever felt certain—especially not romance or intimacy. For me, life up until that point, and for many years thereafter, felt like navigating a minefield of social expectations without a compass.

I grew up in a small New England town before there were such wonders as an internet, an Information Age, or any way for me to know that there were other people like me—people who didn't understand why they felt so out of place in their body. In fact, if you want a depiction of where I grew up, just watch the film *Little Women*, and imagine it with cars and electricity. People's mindsets, however, remained firmly rooted in colonial times.

Oh, and lawnmowers. We had those, too. I remember mowing the front lawn of my house, pushing this deafening, exhaust-spewing monstrosity up the hill where my home was perched. As I labored, I felt something beyond teenage resentment at being forced into menial chores. I felt wrong in my very being. I remember thinking that I must have been a woman in a past life, wishing with bone-deep intensity that I had been born female. Pushing that damn lawnmower was just adding insult to injury.

I had other thoughts of "wrongness" about myself: that I was out of sync with time, born ten years too early or too late. Or maybe I'd been sent to the wrong planet entirely, because nothing about this one felt like home. On summer nights, I'd lie on the asphalt of the cul-de-sac where I grew up, staring up at the stars. The heat of the day still radiated from the pavement as I searched for a tiny, insignificant point of light. Fixing on it, I'd wish with all my heart to be there—anywhere but this small, backwater planet. I was exhausted by the casual cruelty of my peers, the indifference of my elders, and the overwhelming sense that life was about surviving the pain in the hope of a cosmic do-over; that in my next life, I'd be born on the right planet, in the right body, at the right time.

Suffice it to say, I lacked the confidence that "other boys" seemed to have when it came to asking girls out on dates. "Petrified to the point of freezing in place" might be a more accurate description. But that didn't mean I didn't have "girl" friends. I'm sure it won't surprise anyone in the transfeminine community to hear that I had more female friends than male ones. I had an easy rapport with girls, though I didn't understand why at the time.

Even after Sarah and I got married, social gatherings revealed my discomfort in traditionally masculine spaces. At parties, I'd often end up with the men—on the patio, around the cooler or the grill, or in the living room watching the game. I hated it. Every time another bro joined the group, the predictable questions began, and they were mind-numbing. I'd inwardly plead, *Please don't ask me about fantasy football—I couldn't care less*, or *I don't want to talk about work, because I hate it; it's how I hide from all of you.* Sometimes I'd have these moments of derealization where the sound of their voices would fade to monosyllabic tones, and I felt like an alien observer in a host body trying to make sense of this primitive culture. I'd watch their animated discussions about investments or self-driving Teslas and think, *If I could just decipher the linguistic key to this strange culture, maybe I'd understand.* But enlightenment never came, and I'd often snap out of my dissociation just in time to hear someone boasting about their solar panels or the latest tech startup.

There's a scene in the movie *Aliens* where a team of marines discovers a colonist wrapped inside a cocoon in an alien hive. The pale, sickly looking colonist appears to be unconscious until her eyes flash open and she begs, "Please . . . kill me," moments before an alien violently rips its way out of her abdomen. That scene perfectly captures how I felt every time I found myself stuck in a group of men.

Eventually, I would excuse myself and head to the kitchen, seeking solace in Sarah's company. There, the women would talk about their children, sharing funny, surprising, or embarrassing stories. I'd feel an immediate sense of relief. I understood this kind of interaction. It was the type of emotional connection I could relate to. Before long, I'd join the conversation with a story about our daughter, and the women would laugh, nod, or gasp in response. It felt wonderful.

But my presence as a man didn't go unnoticed. Before long, someone would excuse themselves to check on their kids, another would see if the food was ready, and someone else would head to the bathroom. My arrival always disrupted the sacredness of their space, like someone had thrown tear gas into the room. Even Sarah would leave to seek out one of the other women who had slipped away. This was the standard operating procedure of my life for the twelve-plus years we were together.

Denial works best when it's all-encompassing. Social situations were just a small part of a much larger issue. Anything associated with masculinity felt clumsy and awkward to me, and this extended to my relationship with sexual intimacy. During our twelve-year marriage, if I had to guess the number of times Sarah and I had sex, I'd put it well below one hundred. I couldn't say for certain, because sex was something I actively avoided. Even now, it feels shameful to admit that I could not confront my discomfort with sex.

The obvious question might be whether I was attracted to men. In fact, some of the girls I dated before Sarah thought I might be gay. I even ended a relationship with a girl because I grew weary of her persistent questioning about it. But as much as I denied my gender identity, I always knew I wasn't attracted to men. That didn't happen until after I started taking hormones—but I digress.

Since around the time I entered puberty, I fantasized about what it might feel like to be a woman. Where most men fantasize about being with the women in *Playboy* magazine, I imagined myself wearing what they wore: silk negligees, lace teddies, or leather corsets. I was more aroused by the thought of undressing to reveal a feminine body than by the thought of being a man engaging sexually with a woman.

Unfortunately, this extended to the bedroom with Sarah. I cared far more about her pleasure than my own. If I could have satisfied her without using that particular part of my body that felt so uncomfortable to me, I would have. When I was called upon to perform my "husbandly duties," I relied on a variety of coping mechanisms to get through it. I wanted her to be happy, but I rarely climaxed myself, which she interpreted as an unspoken commentary on her desirability as a woman. Sometimes I even faked orgasms, telling her it was a "small one" and I was satisfied. Other times, I'd say I'd become oversensitized and couldn't continue. It was my version of the "it's not you, it's me" story. My most-used coping mechanism, however, was fantasizing that I was a woman during the act. Years later, I learned this phenomenon is called sexual dissociation. In my case, it was how I tried to find pleasure in something most men sought out eagerly.

In hindsight, I'm shocked at how much denial shaped my life. The signs of my gender dysphoria were as glaring as being hit with a two-by-four, but I remained oblivious, even when I got knocked down the metaphorical stairs.

However, it wasn't just denial. Before Sarah and I married, I tried to open up to her about my desire to explore my femininity. She drew a line in the sand, making it clear that if I crossed it, she would leave.

If not her, then what?

In the summer of 2004, Sarah and I went to see a relationship counselor, at my insistence. My reasons were simple: I was dissatisfied with the banality of our sexual relationship. I also felt immense shame about my desire for broader sexual expression in the bedroom, but I knew from experience that being direct with Sarah often led to defensiveness and inflexibility. I hoped that speaking in the presence of a professional might soften her stance, or at least encourage her to meet me halfway.

In our session, I tentatively explained how I wanted to explore my femininity and overcome the shame I carried. I said I wanted to create space for greater self-expression, not just for me but for both of us. It was a vulnerable plea for intimacy.

Unfortunately, Sarah didn't waver. She stated unequivocally that she wanted no part of it and would leave if I pursued it. The counselor responded, "It seems she's being pretty clear about what she wants. You'll have to decide what you want." I couldn't imagine transitioning alone, let alone what kind of life I might have if I did.

Looking back, it saddens me to realize that I locked a part of myself away that day. Both Sarah and the counselor sent the same message: It wasn't okay to be my authentic self. I was told to choose: Either be myself and face fear, scarcity, and loss, or conform to their expectations and keep Sarah's love. It wasn't a fair choice, nor was it compassionate toward the struggles I faced with my gender identity.

Now, with the perspective I've gained, I feel angry because I was forced to make a decision where I lost either way. Sarah and the counselor perpetuated my suffering because I didn't fit their narrow definition of what was acceptable. Their complacency left me ashamed, and I buried my feelings even deeper. I had to deny the existence of the feminine part of myself. But, as with all things we repress, those feelings found unhealthy ways to manifest.

Denying my femininity created a fissure in my mind—a curiosity that, at times, grew into an obsession. With the help of the internet, I began secretly exploring what it meant to be transgender. "What did hormones do?" I wondered. "Could I really grow breasts? Wait, you can have a real vagina? I thought they just cut *it* off." I learned that many of the transphobic myths I'd heard were baseless. And the truth was undeniable: I wanted breasts—desperately.

But I couldn't bring myself to go to a doctor for a prescription. Shame held me back, as did fears of sterility. I did want to have children someday. If I did grow breasts, what kind of a life would I have? How would I earn a living? Fear, loss, and scarcity dominated my thinking. Still, the pressure to explore persisted.

I became active on a message board for people who were questioning their gender or transitioning. That's where I learned about herbal estrogen. Who needed a prescription, when all I needed was a supplement that could give me breasts? The supplement had reviews like, "Omg these are amazing—two bra sizes in just two months!" What could possibly go wrong?

Hesitantly, I ordered a tincture containing phytoestrogen-rich herbs like saw palmetto, *Pueraria mirifica*, and black cohosh. If the online reviews were to be believed, I could expect to grow breasts in as little as six weeks! The illogic of my thinking at that time now baffles me. I told myself I would just try it, and if I started to grow breasts I would stop. I just wanted to see if anything would happen. Seriously, if I could yell back at myself across the rift of decades, I would scream at my former self, "Girl! You are trans! Stop denying it!" So deep was my denial, though, that even if I could have heard my future self back then, I wouldn't have believed her.

For six months, I kept ordering bottles, hoping for results. Maybe with this next bottle, something magical would start to happen. But without something to block my testosterone production, I was fighting an uphill battle.

Unfortunately, Sarah found one of my bottles and confronted me about it. Of course, I couldn't reveal that I was trying to develop breasts; she would have left me if I did. I panicked and gave her a half-truth: I said I was trying to increase my nipple sensitivity. Though she hesitantly believed me, she insisted I stop taking it. That marked the end of my herbal estrogen experiments, and it would be twelve long years before I tried taking hormones again.

If not her, then when?

One of my favorite stories concerns the origin of my name, Calista. When I was fifteen, I bought a video game for my Commodore 64 (yes, I just dated myself). It was a dungeon crawler called *The Bard's Tale*. It was the first game I owned that allowed you to choose a character's name and gender. This choice felt significant. Some embryonic part of me knew that I wasn't just naming a character; I was creating an alter ego.

Inspired by my love of astronomy, I turned to books on the subject for ideas. In one, I found the names of the moons of Jupiter. Among their names, one stuck out: Callisto. Named after a nymph of Artemis, Callisto is finally transformed into a bear and sent to the heavens as Ursa Major, the constellation we call the Big Dipper. Given my desire to be cast off this planet and live among the stars, it was the obvious choice. Callisto became a part of me, existing in some small recess of my mind.

Over time, Callisto evolved into Calista, a name that felt softer and more feminine. And to this day, I won't play any game that forces me to play as a male character. Calista became my avatar in every video game I played, but as I grew older, I began to wonder: Was she more than just an alter ego?

When I was thirty-two, I decided to find out. I wanted to know if Calista was more than just a figment of my imagination. So I decided I would stop mentally suppressing her and give her permission to "come out" if she was truly there.

I was home alone in the apartment Sarah and I shared. It was a sunny day, and a warm breeze blew through the open window and down the corridor leading back to the bedroom. Lying on our bed, I closed my eyes and thought to myself, *Calista, if you're really there, it's okay for you to come out.* After the briefest of pauses, I felt a pressure building—an awareness in my consciousness, like a door long closed to some inner recess of my mind had just been unlocked. What follows is, quite truthfully, how I have come to understand my experience, rendered in screenplay form:

```
CUT TO:
INT. CASTLE, DUNGEON—DAY

WIDE SHOT of a bleak, dark, sullen place. A single
ray of light from a hole high up in the stonework
pierces the gloom. ECHOES of the living world can
be heard from outside, but the hole is too high up
and far away for anything to be clearly discerned.
In this place the walls themselves radiate pain
and sadness. No vermin are present; it's too
depressing for even them. But there is something
here, barely visible in the darkness.

A DISHEVELED FIGURE rests with their back against
one wall, their arms wrapped around their knees.
Whoever they are, they've been here long enough to
have become a fixture of their surroundings.

Opposite them, on the far wall, a sturdy IRON DOOR
remains closed, barring any chance of escape.
```

A mechanical CLICK comes from the door, and a moment later, with a CREAK and a GROAN the door slowly swings open.

Back to the WIDE SHOT: We see that the ray of sunlight now extends past the open door, inviting the dungeon’s occupant to leave.

The figure wakes slowly from their semiconscious state. They raise their head, revealing the face of a WOMAN. She stares at the open door, not trusting what she’s seeing.

Slowly, she pulls herself to her feet, and with trepidation, she walks towards the open door.

INT. CASTLE, DUNGEON CORRIDOR—DAY

The stone corridor is empty and extends into darkness. There’s no way to know how long she has been here, or how many others have been resigned to their fate in this place.

On the LEFT, from the open doorway, the beam of sunlight cuts diagonally across the frame, a spot of light illuminating the center of the floor, just outside the cell.

The sounds of the woman's shuffling feet can be heard as she enters the frame, breaking the beam of light. She shuffles her way to the center of the hallway, the light now resting above her dirty feet.

She pauses there, slowly looking around in bewilderment. If we could hear her thoughts, she’d be thinking, Where are the guards?

Her head turns toward us; she sees something.

REVERSE ANGLE to see from behind the woman that stairs lead up and to the LEFT, out of this terrible place.

In a burst of speed, SHE RUNS towards the stairs.

CUT TO:
INT. CASTLE, THRONE ROOM—DAY

This is a fortress of a room composed of large, chiseled blocks of gray granite. It's austere in its adornments, but crimson TAPESTRIES break up the monotony of the walls.

Large CHANDELIERS descend from an unseen ceiling, their myriad candles illuminating a crimson RUG flanked on each side by TWELVE GUARDS, six to a side. They stand at attention in full uniform, each holding a PIKE upright. This tableau forms converging lines leading to a dais with an ornate THRONE.

Sitting upon the throne is THE MAD KING. He looks old, tired, and frail. A jeweled CROWN rests atop a skull covered in long strands of white hair, and a white beard descends to the middle of his chest. He mumbles to himself incoherently.

The Mad King should have abdicated the throne long ago, but his spite for others, his self-hatred, and his fear of losing control have kept him alive.

The Mad King continues to mumble incoherently until abruptly, he stops. He's become aware of something beyond the senses.

His eyes search back and forth. His thoughts regain a semblance of awareness. His eyes FLASH wide with realization.

Like the creak and groan of the dungeon door opening, the Mad King inhales slowly with a long RASP of air.

He's about to speak when a SCREAM can be heard in the distance—faintly at first, but growing louder by the moment.

INT. CASTLE, THRONE HALL—DAY

A long hall with a red carpet extends into the distance. White light radiates from a large window at the far end of the hall. Hundreds of framed PAINTINGS line the walls.

The woman from the dungeon, Calista, enters the frame from the RIGHT. Without a stumble, she rounds the corner heading directly for the throne room—screaming for vengeance!

INT. CASTLE, THRONE ROOM—DAY

She's about to enter the room when the Mad King finds his voice.

MAD KING

Guards! Stop her! STOP HER!

On his order, the guards extend their pikes across the path to the Mad King, blocking any further progress.

Calista CRASHES into the pikes, but they do not budge.

CALISTA

(screaming)

No! Let me through!

MAD KING

(stammering)

Take—take her! Take her away!

The two foremost guards forcefully grab Calista by her arms. She fights to get free, but it's no use. The guards easily overpower her.

Calista cries out in tears as the guards drag her by her heels down the hallway.

```
The Mad King watches as they take her away. He's
visibly disturbed and fights for composure.

                    MAD KING
              (mumbling to himself)

     My kingdom . . . it's mine! My kingdom.

We hold on the fear-stricken king's face as we

FADE TO BLACK.
```

I sprang up off of my bed in a panic. I thought, *Am I having a panic attack? I've never had a panic attack!* I checked my self-awareness. *I am having a panic attack!* Never before in my life had I experienced anxiety like this. It was a completely foreign feeling, and it scared the hell out of me. There was only one course of action for me to take: suppress, repress, and forget it ever happened.

The fear of what it meant was too much to bear. I did not want this for myself. However, I now knew that Calista was real, and I would spend the next twelve years doing everything I could to forget about her, lying to myself about who I was: the Mad King who would rule their kingdom in sickness. But Calista was far more clever than the Mad King realized. Other parts of myself had seen her, and those parts would secretly visit her in the dungeon. Calista would whisper ideas to them, and they would spread the message like a virus: "The Queen lives! The Queen lives!"

If not her, then where?

Moving forward from the experience of Calista's summoning, I refocused my attention on what was actually possible; getting married, having kids, working hard, creating the future I thought I wanted. Yet, despite my efforts, I couldn't forget what I experienced.

As a child who was assigned male at birth, the promise of a successful life had been passed down to me by my parents, as it had been passed down to them by theirs. It was the promise of expectation, societal conditioning, and domestication: Go to school, get a job, work hard, build wealth, get married, buy a house, have kids, send them to college, retire comfortably, and bask in the accomplishments of a life well-lived. Rinse and repeat, world without end, whoever has the most toys wins.

I had the toys—a lot of them. But the funny thing was, the more things I owned, the more depressed I became. Each accomplishment only compounded the lie I was trying to convince myself was true.

I remember vividly that shortly after the birth of our daughter, Sarah entered the nesting phase of our domestic life. Fortunately, I had been making good money as a freelance editor for film and television. We found a house we could afford in a nice suburb of Los Angeles (with good schools, of course). The house was bank-owned, which meant it needed repairs. Luckily, I was handy with all sorts of tools. One of the biggest projects was cleaning and resurfacing the pool. I remember thinking, "How hard can it be?"

To set the scene, this was late 2008, just as the housing crisis was about to bottom out. A recession was underway, and the studios and networks were scaling back their budgets. This meant fewer projects were being developed, and fewer jobs for a tradesman like me. I found myself out of work, running out of money, with a mortgage, a newborn daughter, and a stay-at-home mom to support. And there I was, standing at the bottom of an empty pool—a literal hole in the ground—wondering how I was going to climb out. I was scared, depressed, and felt financially unsupported.

Looking back now, I wish I had understood something important about Sarah: She didn't want to work on anyone else's terms but her own. She dreamed of being a traditional housewife, and I don't resent her for that. She's been a good mother to our daughter, and that has paid dividends for our child's well-being. However, there was never an understanding between us that I would have to be the sole breadwinner for the family. I resented being pushed even further into the stereotypical role of a 1950s husband and father—a role I never would have agreed to if I had been asked.

As I stood in the bottom of that pool, I told myself that this was what "happily ever after" looked like. That *this* was normal, and I just needed to accept it. That life would never get any better than this.

There's a scene in the movie *I Saw the TV Glow* that perfectly illustrates this feeling. The main character, Owen, has just bought a new TV and is bringing it into the house. In voiceover, he says, "He has a family of his own now, whom he loves more than anything." Yet we never see the family; only the loneliness and isolation of playing the role of husband and father. While the movie came out in 2024, the eerie similarity of that scene to what my life had become before I transitioned chilled me to my core. This was the agreement I had made with myself: choosing to exist instead of truly living.

If not her, then why?

After twelve years of denial, I had reached the end of my rope. I was drinking more frequently, isolating myself from social engagements, and preferring to be alone. Meanwhile, Sarah and my daughter spent time bonding in the living room. I increasingly retreated to the spare bedroom, spending hours engrossed in video games.

It should be said that video games offer a safe refuge from the harsh reality of life for many trans people. For me, a transgender woman in denial, video games allowed me to explore my femininity in a safe environment where I could fully be the woman I couldn't yet be in real life. Nowhere was this truer than in the virtual world of *Second Life*. In *Second Life*, the character creation and customization options seemed endless, from dozens of face and body shape controls to thousands of skin color and texture combinations. Countless hairstyles could be purchased, not to mention a near infinite variety of clothing options. Through this platform, I lived out shopping fantasies impossible to achieve in real life. Unlike traditional video games, *Second Life* had no predefined goal. You could be whoever you wanted and go wherever you wished. It became my proving ground for practicing my femininity.

One evening, Sarah came into the spare bedroom to talk to me while I was playing. She didn't know about *Second Life*; it was my secret, and a source of shame. When I heard her approaching, I quickly switched to another video game I had minimized in the taskbar.

Sarah sat on the edge of the bed as I remained at my desk. She told me my gaming habits were affecting how she felt about me. I remember hearing what she said, but it didn't seem to matter. I don't recall my exact reply, but I know that, in that moment, I didn't care how my behavior was affecting her. This was my refuge; in the terms of *I Saw the TV Glow*, gaming was my connection to the Pink Opaque while I was living in the Midnight Realm. Stopping was unthinkable. She might as well have asked me to stop breathing.

I couldn't stop, nor could I tell her why. Years ago, she had made it clear that sharing my truth wasn't safe. So I simply told her I wasn't going to stop. Sarah nodded, said "Okay," and left the room. I knew I had made a mistake, but I didn't know what else to do. My despair was near its breaking point, yet I still couldn't let go. The Mad King's bony hands held a death grip on the throne even as his kingdom burned.

Years later, Sarah told me that was the moment she decided to stop prioritizing my needs over her own. But it wasn't my needs she had been supporting; she has always put her comfort with living an average, mediocre life first. It was the fantasy of a happy, heterosexual marriage that she had been trying to maintain. Sarah confessed that she even prayed to God—despite being agnostic—for me to become more masculine.

The final blow came in early 2017. I had been editing a new series, but when that job came to an end, I couldn't find more work. The television industry was evolving, favoring younger, cheaper, less experienced workers, and I was tired: tired of chasing jobs, tired of pretending to care about a career that drained me, and most of all, tired of showing up for others while feeling empty inside. The Mad King's breathing became heavy and labored, his strength faltering. Meanwhile, like Sarah Connor in *Terminator 2: Judgment Day*, Calista used her time in captivity to grow stronger. She couldn't be contained much longer.

In September of 2017 I had been looking online for clarity, searching for answers to the question: "How to know if you're transgender?" A YouTube video titled *Common Excuses to Avoid Transitioning* caught my eye. Every excuse I had used for years was there: "I won't be passable." "I'm too muscular." "I'm too old to transition." But it wasn't this list of my own excuses that struck a chord with me. It was what the host said next: "The trans woman who may not be passable, but is in public nevertheless, is likely to find herself happier than the woman who is not out." It was a mic-drop moment. That night, I reached out to the video's creator, a therapist name Alexis, seeking help untangling the scrambled ball of wiring my brain had become.

I was relieved when Alexis responded, and I booked a couple of online sessions with her. During the first one, I shared a list of pros and cons about why I may or may not be transgender. In the second session, I asked her outright: "Am I trans?" Her response was simple: "You're checking off all the right boxes." I broke down in tears for what felt like an hour. Finally, someone had validated the truth I had been denying all my life. Wiping away my tears, I asked her, "What's next?"

The next step was coming out to Sarah. Alexis told me she wouldn't write me a letter for hormone therapy until I did so. In hindsight, this was highly unethical. Forcing me to reveal something so delicate under duress created risks for my family and me. It was like dangling a carrot on a stick in front of a pig; I felt compelled to move where she directed me.

I decided to write Sarah a letter, pouring onto paper thoughts and feelings that had been trapped inside me. I explained my depression, my withdrawal, and my escape into video games. I shared how my fear of her rejecting me had kept my truth hidden, even from myself. I ended with a plea to preserve our marriage and family. After printing the letter, I read over my words, then crumpled it into a ball and tossed it in the trash. I wasn't ready. It wasn't the right time.

Even without hormones, acknowledging my truth lifted my long suffering despair. For the first time, I wasn't pretending to be someone else. I was seeing things from the other side of the looking glass—no longer trying to project a façade of what I thought people wanted to see, but instead projecting a genuine representation of who I truly was. With this growing self-awareness, a confidence that I hadn't felt in years emerged. Sarah also noticed this positive change in me.

On a Sunday afternoon, after Sarah and I had lunch with her mother, she came into the spare bedroom where I was playing a game. As Sarah tells it, she wanted to connect more with me because she felt more connected to me than she had in a long while. She settled on the edge of the bed and began sharing her thoughts from the day. I don't know what came over me—perhaps it was her pleasant demeanor—but I reached into the trash can and retrieved the crumpled letter, handing it to her to read.

Now, I didn't just hand her a wadded-up ball of paper and say, "Here, read this." I'm quite certain that I explained that I had been working on a letter for her to read but was unsure how to present it to her. Sarah uncrumpled the paper. As she read, I couldn't help but feel a sense of dread, wondering if I had made a grave mistake. The silence in the room felt heavy, like a jury about to deliver their verdict. Would I be acquitted and loved? Or found guilty and banished for my actions?

As she finished reading the letter, she slowly nodded, then pursed her lips. What say you, the jury, in the case of your husband and father of your child revealing that they're a woman of transgender experience? Her response: "I'm shocked, but I'm not surprised."

What followed was a long conversation about the future. I expressed my desire to begin hormone therapy, which Sarah strongly opposed. However, I reasoned that throughout my life, I had explored numerous avenues in pursuit of happiness, only to encounter dead ends at every turn. What if this was the missing part that finally made me feel whole? It was an argument she couldn't ignore. I had to at least try and see what happened.

Reluctantly, Sarah asked me to wait until after her upcoming yoga retreat in Greece. I agreed, though it was excruciating to delay what I hoped would be my path to freedom. However, I didn't squander this time. While Sarah was away, I met with an endocrinologist about starting gender-affirming hormone therapy.

By the time Sarah returned, I had a supply of estradiol tablets and spironolactone in my medicine cabinet. Every time I looked at the pills, they had a seductive pull on me, urging me to start taking them. However, I had promised Sarah that I wouldn't until she returned. I would close the door to the cabinet and try to suppress the urge for a little while longer.

The day after Sarah returned, I informed her that I was prepared to begin hormone therapy. She seemed taken aback by this revelation. Perhaps she had hoped I had forgotten about the whole matter, or maybe she thought she could pretend I'd never mentioned it. Yet, once again, I had to explain why trying hormones was essential for me, acknowledging that while this might not be the ultimate answer, I wouldn't know unless I tried. Reluctantly, Sarah acknowledged what I had said, but she didn't agree or condone it. This lukewarm response was the closest thing to approval I was likely to receive. The date was October 15, 2017.

In the movie *Pleasantville*, the occupants live in a black-and-white world of suburban America, circa 1950. Their entire social order, as well as their individual lives, is confined to a repetitive existence of blissful ignorance—that is, until a woman from another world arrives and shows the citizens all the color, beauty, and depth that they have been missing. Six days after I started hormone therapy, my own world transformed from one that was drab and lifeless to one where I could finally see and feel the richness life had to offer. I vividly remember saying to myself out loud, "Oh! So this is why people like being alive." I had finally found what had been missing all my life. I believe that the combination of not having to pretend to be someone I wasn't and the hormones that my brain and body had needed to function properly made the biggest difference. Finally, at long last, Calista was set free.

Sarah, however, was unwilling to accept my newfound sense of self. She moved out of our bedroom, choosing instead to sleep in the other room. Phone calls, once made openly, became discreet and secretive. Worse still, she told her mother, along with six of her friends, about my transition without my knowledge. Unbeknownst to me at the time, Sarah was already sowing the seeds of her departure. Her indifference towards me only grew with time. She seemed to lose all empathy. I remember remarking on how cold she had become, how it felt like I didn't even know who she was anymore. Her response was chilling: She said she was moving on, and shutting her emotions down was the only way she could get through this process.

I share in the blame for her emotional detachment, though. While Sarah was grieving the loss of her husband and the life she had planned for herself, Calista was coming into her own. I felt more alive than I had at any point since childhood, and I plunged into my transition with abandon. So brazen was I that, according to Sarah, I told her I wanted to have a funeral for my old self. Now, while I have no recollection of ever saying this, and in all likelihood only meant it in some small, personal way for myself, Sarah took it to literally mean that I wanted a full-on funeral with guests and a casket. The point I'm trying to illustrate here is that Sarah and I were now diametrically opposed to each other in terms of what each of us wanted with respect to my transition.

The therapist I was seeing at the time referred to having two types of clients when it came to transition: cheetahs and sloths. I may have been slow in accepting my truth, but once there, I broke every speed record I could for transitioning. I wanted Sarah to keep up with me, but I ended up leaving her in the dust without ever looking back. In hindsight, I could have moved forward in my transition with less enthusiasm, being more empathetic and thoughtful about what Sarah was going through. Perhaps, if I had eased into it more slowly, been more compassionate to Sarah, our marriage may have pulled through. Though I've also wondered: Did I love Sarah, or did I love that I was able to hide my truth with her for as long as I did?

In January 2018, Sarah told me she was moving out and wanted a divorce. At the time, I clung to the hope that she would come around and that we could rebuild our life together. Looking back now, I realize there was never any chance of that happening. I have often said that in that moment, my heart broke into a thousand million pieces.

Years earlier, at Sarah's bridal party, her friends had called me to ask a series of questions to see how well I knew my bride-to-be. One of the questions asked which song best described Sarah. I don't remember the other options, but I picked "I'd Do Anything for Love (But I Won't Do That)" by Meat Loaf. It was the correct answer then, and it feels just as fitting now.

My story is a cautionary tale of wasted years and what could never have been. I now see how strongly fear dictated my decisions for so long. When I review all the moments where I tried to express my femininity, it seems so obvious that I was—and always have been—a woman. I can only shake my head in disbelief at how long I lived in denial. I literally just asked myself, "How the hell did you not know?!" But deep down, I think I always knew. I simply put it off for as long as I could.

No one wakes up one day and says, "Hey! I think I'll transition. It'll be fun!" I wanted an easy-breezy, happy life, and transitioning is hard. But when I decided to transition, I reimagined what was possible for myself. I went back to school for my master's degree and began a new career as a psychotherapist. I've had numerous surgeries to undo the years of testosterone poisoning I endured, and when I look in the mirror now, I can't help but smile at my reflection. I see the woman who was there all along, patiently waiting for her time to come.

One of my favorite expressions is "I've never met a strong person with an easy past." That sentiment resonates deeply with me. From enduring a difficult childhood, to creating a life based on the expectations of others, to finally confronting and overcoming my own denial, I have emerged stronger and happier than ever. Even Sarah confessed that she now sees that I was living my life at 25 percent of what it is now. Today I can truly say that I am happy inside and out. Because of that, I hope to spend the rest of my life making the world a little better than I found it.

The Stretch and Break of Becoming

TERÉ FOWLER-CHAPMAN

I stood in front of the mirror as the weight of becoming what had once lived only within me began appearing in my reflection. I think it was this moment, in between rushed T shots before Sara came home, that I realized my marriage would never work. This recognition haunted me, dancing between the lines of conversations with my best friend; between the booming silence in moments she no longer wanted to be a part of; and in the mirror, between the newfound chin hairs I was plucking after she described them as grotesque. It was too real and surreal simultaneously. *How did we get here?*

When we met, I was at the height of my career as a poet and organizer in a small city. I was with my first girlfriend at the time, and Sara was a regular listener at the open mic I started. She later told me she had long been attracted to my dreadlocks, my smile, and the poetic night all at once. I was too wrapped up in my first out queer relationship to see the signs she was throwing my way. I was too busy creating a name for myself that stood beyond just being the romantic partner of the best dancer in town. That's the thing about a small town: It carries a type of magic that allows you to be whoever you say you are.

So I was a poet, who I always said I would be. I founded Words on the Avenue, the first open mic of its kind, in downtown Tucson, Arizona. I was slowly leaning into my childhood dreams as an adult and debunking what I thought I was supposed to be at the same time. Outside my artistry, I was shifting in my gender identity too. When the dancer and I first met, I was draped in yarn braids, committed to long skirts, a good red lip, and sundresses. Over time, the dancer taught me how to tie a tie, called me by my masculine name when it felt safe for me to call myself Troy, and encouraged me to shop in the men's section when I thought skinny jeans, a women's button-up, and a bow tie were my only options. When I discovered the dancer was cheating, I was heartbroken and in denial until she let me go. Through this dynamic of acceptance and infidelity, dance and poetry, weed and liquor, love and loss, I learned that my identity was not just tied to my roles or relationships; rather, it was something deeply personal and ever evolving.

This story isn't just about the beginning; it is also about an ending that felt like a beginning too. But to start with my ex-wife, I have to start with my first girlfriend, because when that relationship was ending, my friendship with my ex-wife was deepening. When I first met Sara in the sea of community that would pile into that coffee shop to hear poems at the end of every month, it was raining. When I first talked to Sara, she immediately shared that her brother was battling addiction and that she was struggling in school. The first time Sara texted me, she apologized for disclosing her brother's shortcomings. The first time I texted back, I encouraged her vulnerability. When Sara first saw me, I was dating someone I needed to be with. When I first saw Sara, I was struggling with letting go of my first love. When I first met Sara, I didn't drink a lot, but I did drink often; when I first met Sara, she had her first glass of wine. After the first conversation with Sara, I wanted her to stay, but I didn't want the dancer to go, even though the dancer was gone already.

I called it cheating, abandonment, reasons to drink, reasons to fuck, an age gap—I called it everything except what it truly was. I never called it sadness, time, space, or shame. As Sara and I grew closer, we bonded over grief and loss. She was grieving her brother without saying much about it. I was grieving a heartbreak from a love neither one of my parents accepted. I'm not sure how it really began, but I do know the dancer saw it first in the midst of our ambiguous breakup. Sara and I were sitting in the coffee shop when the dancer called. I introduced Sara as my friend, and the dancer said, "I knew it, the way you looked at her. I could see it; it was something."

With Sara I often felt a sense of colorism and misogynoir from our small city, which immediately embraced the idea of my relationship with a multiracial person (Sara) in a way that two dark-skinned queer people in love didn't receive, despite the dancer and me investing more talent into the community as a couple than Sara and I ever did. I ignored the discomfort by feeding into the comfort and eventually fed into the idea of who we were to everyone else, instead of who we were to one another. When Sara struggled to follow her inner compass, I invested in her dreams. Together, we became a local power couple put on a local pedestal, and I enjoyed it immensely. I grew smaller and more conscious when she insisted I was flirting with someone I wasn't thinking twice about. I unapologetically stood in the face of my Black friends when she said they were being racist toward her multiracial identity, and I centered her pain instead of centering their confusion. Without realizing it, my gender and sexuality, which I had so freely celebrated with the dancer, became of little importance to me. I was evolving and seeking pleasure, I was changing and fawning, and I was decentering myself to comfort her.

During the foundation of our relationship, The Orange was running for president the first time, and I was afraid of losing the right to marry. I was afraid of dying and being buried as a woman, and I was also afraid of living as my authentic self. I was afraid of time, and I was afraid of wasting it; our early twenties had passed, and we were still together. I asked her mom for her hand in marriage. When she said yes, I gave her the date I would propose to Sara. As that date neared, her mom called me and asked if I had done it yet. When I began backtracking, her mom ushered me forward. On a train from Tucson to New Orleans, I was in the bathroom getting approval from her dad while Sara kept a young Black pastor—who was enamored with our love—company. When we arrived in NOLA, I dropped to one knee in the Airbnb, and after she said yes, I immediately called her mom. It was done, and I wasn't sure why I'd done it that way. The hurried feelings and pressure were the last thing Sara mentioned as we looked out onto the Mississippi River before hopping back on the train to head home. I felt a sense of honor to have the option of having a human right, and I felt afraid of having that right taken away. I felt a sense of letting people down, and I felt a sense of being too young but too old at the same time. Our marriage temporarily eased these anxieties, but it wasn't the antidote. A year later, I was desensitized to a deep-rooted calling when she called me "wife" far too often and for far too long. Initially, marriage did provide a sense of legitimacy and normalcy, particularly in the eyes of society. I felt like I had succeeded in escaping the statistics of a broken home. I felt like others were proud of me and I was on track with the American Dream, maybe even ahead a little bit. However, divorce shattered that façade, revealing that true legitimacy comes from within, not from external validation.

I swallowed the first sign of trouble. Most nights, I was just like the phases of the moon, shifting, redefining; but unlike the moon, I was always being questioned for it. Together, we were wrapped in a warped silence that was threatened at the thought of sharing ideas that differed and disappointed each other. Instead, my work became financial lifts that carried my bitterness and resentment along with us through times of hardship. She didn't say much about my beliefs and activism, but I knew how she felt when she brought me a shirt that said "100% Human" that had been sold to raise money for an All Lives Matter campaign. The campaign was a response to the birth of the Black Lives Matter movement, after young Black people, like Trayvon Martin and Michael Brown, were killed. I was an androgynous secret during these times, full of compromise. People were asking my pronouns out of respect, and I was too afraid to answer.

I asked her, "If I transitioned, would you still love me?"

"I don't know," she answered honestly. "I don't know."

Even if I did want to transition, I didn't feel like I could say it; even if I could say it, I didn't feel like I had anyone to say it to. I wish this was my coming-of-age story. Bits of it are, but I wish it was more than bits. I wish it was whole. One day when we were riding in the back of an SUV after visiting Bisbee, Arizona, for a blues festival, I was reading *The Argonauts* by Maggie Nelson when I realized for the first time that love and transitioning were not mutually exclusive. Some transmen had both! After reading the final page of that book, I wrote in a notebook, "I'm going to transition," and handed it to her. She read it and returned the notebook emotionlessly, and she stared out the window for the rest of the ride home. A bit of my becoming is also in *Middlesex* by Jeffrey Eugenides, a book at my mother's house. Unbeknownst to my mom, I read it over and over again, seeing my young self in something I didn't have the words to describe.

A bit of coming of age emerged when I ran around shirtless until I was twelve, when my father told me, "You have bong bongs [breasts]; we get it. Now put them away!" I didn't understand, but I never walked around with a towel around my hips until I was off on my own. I also didn't understand when a bit of the becoming came forward in fourth grade after sex-ed class, when I told a classmate, "I want to be a boy because I don't want to be pregnant; I want to get people pregnant," and she ran away like I had cooties, yelling "Ewww!" I liked the bits of that bit, having cooties. A few little bits surfaced when the dancer said, "I taught you how to tie it, and now you wear that tie every day. I really loved it, but it's yours." Pulling it up close to my neck, meeting my wry smile with one of her own. One of the last bits burst through every time Sara wanted something or wanted to go somewhere, and I happily and financially obliged because I thought good men ought to. She supported all the bits but my medical transition. She supported the chest binder bits, the perfect strap-on bits, the bits of becoming that were hidden to the naked eye. The catalyst was when the bits she didn't support were the bits the gunman saw that day when he pointed the gun at me. I was headed back to work as a high school educator. I had left after school to get a pick-me-up from the gas station across campus. On my way back, I hopped into the crosswalk, and the gunman was ahead of me in the crosswalk. My presence made the gunman nervous—nervous enough to pull out a gun. He saw what some people saw and what Sara refused to see: a Black man.

We didn't talk much about the gunman or about what happened in that crosswalk that Friday either. Just like we didn't talk much about grief or the bits of addiction peeking through me, the bits of sex that centered her pleasure, the bits of her face that frowned at the thought of her pleasuring me. My ongoing evolution to masculinity was created bit by bit, and it was happening before and a bit after the medical assistance. I shoved the gun incident—along with those bits of truth—deep into a crushed empty can of IPA that weekend, and another, and another. The incident happened on a Friday, and by Monday I was in a therapist's office for all the right things but for all the wrong reasons. Sara's silent fears of my becoming slowly began to gather voice, and I didn't know which I preferred more—Sara's quiet or the blatancy in her honesty. She would say, "Do you really want the Muslims in my family to call you *he*?" Or she would say, "My dad isn't going to get it." Or she would say, "No one will know I am gay anymore if you transition." Or she would say, "I don't like men."

Instead of these being signs, they became resentment that stuck to my internal library. They became reasons to drink, and then they became more. I blamed testosterone for my anger, but what I know about testosterone is that it doesn't feed on anger the way resentment does. She wasn't happy I was here. I was here but wasn't happy to be alive. I became obsessed with getting to death before death got to me again. I couldn't start and stop until the drunken stupor was an intelligible pain that was small enough to fit in a glass but became large enough to drown our home and swallow what was left of our joy. The pain manifested in outrage and oversharing and overpouring, and it happened more often than it should have. Addiction and C-PTSD aren't pretty diseases, and the truth is I used the gunman's threat on my life as clear confirmation to get on T. It was my way of silver-lining the trauma, like I had always done in the past, but this one was too big to be drawn over.

The reality is, when your life is threatened for being Black in America, the only thing you feel is the feeling of never mattering at all. A threat against life for being Black and alive opens an overwhelming wound that infects all the deepest traumas around it. The wound becomes larger, and the hole becomes so wide and wild that nothing can fill it—not authenticity, not silence, not liquor, not passion, not poems, not lies. I carried so much shame about how I let the white gunman go instead of pressing charges against him for randomly pointing a gun at me in a crosswalk. The shame was heavy, and the anger festered. It was as if my life was roadkill on the side of the street, and the rest of the world was in cars passing by.

I recover loudly now to honor what this past version of myself experienced and carried. I do this because I want people to know that addiction and substance use disorder are not moral failures; they are catastrophic responses to an irnsurmountable amount of pain. The stressors and pain I experienced over my lifetime damaged me significantly and ultimately contributed to my path of self-destruction. Somewhere in the processing of all of the harm and hurt was the divorce.

The word *divorce* was a whisper that took some time to grow sound, and I hated every time I saw it on a form. During the divorce, I lost the stability and companionship of a family and friend I had grown accustomed to. After the divorce, I slowly gained a deeper understanding of my needs, identity, and friendships, along with the importance of solace within myself. During my battle with my addiction, I got accustomed to calling myself an alcoholic and found that easier than saying *Hi my name is ___ and I've been married before* or *Hi my name is ____ and I'm divorced.* I felt like society had given us this gift; and later, when I learned that she had conceived a child with a cisgender man a few months after our separation, I felt like I had fumbled it. Neither of us picked up the divorce process until after my best friend (who was also a close friend of hers) died. I guess I got too lost in all the healing and grief to make the divorce official. When she reached out and asked me to sign the rights over confirming that her child was not mine and to complete the divorce process, I agreed and relived the trauma of our separation. Marriage is not a gift; it's a human right, and it was well within our right to admit we needed to go our separate ways.

Divorce is not a moral failure. It's an overdue right that puts a tremendous amount of pressure on queer people to suppress for the sake of surviving. Now that I'm older and remarried, I know marriage takes work, commitment, honesty, openness, and communication to thrive. My divorce forced me to do the work on myself that needed to be done; it forced me to be whole for me first. Divorce challenged me to say no to misalignment in people, places, and things, and to say yes to environments that cultivated vulnerability, accountability, and warmth. I often tell the humans I work with that we don't learn the most when we feel like we've won; we learn the most when we feel like we've really lost. Be careful about what you call a fumble and what you call victory. Divorce isn't an ending; it's actually a beginning. For me, it was the first step on a journey way beyond what I could have ever imagined in that small town.

Queering Consciously Uncoupling and Recoupling

A Story of Queer Trans Love, Divorce, and Imagining New Ways of Being

SHANNA KATZ KATTARI, PHD, MED, AND
LEONARDO KATTARI, PHD, MSW

"Of all the sex toy stores in all of the world, you happened to walk into this one." We met on December 17, 2008, after Shanna had sat shiva for the recent loss of a cat and ventured back out into the world to teach a Strap-On 101 sex course. Afterward, Leo approached them to ask some questions, validated their femmeness in a way that they had been missing, and the rest, as they say, is history.

As is our marriage. But also, it's not. As a couple (kinda) of queer and trans folks, we are used to disrupting, deconstructing, and reimagining what it looks like to be in relation with the world and with one another. This is our divorce story, though it isn't the story of the end of our relationship.

After a few years together living in both Colorado and Arizona, and ending up back in Denver, we decided to have a Queer Celebration of Love. Neither marriage nor civil unions were legal in Colorado at the time, so legal recognition wasn't even a consideration. Rather, we invited all of our friends and the family who were willing to support us, hired our favorite rainbow-'hawked DJ, ordered a variety of cupcakes (including gluten-free vegan ones—this WAS a queer wedding!) from our favorite cupcake shop, and hosted the queer gothic Victorian fall-themed celebration of our dreams. This is the anniversary we celebrate; this is where we shared our commitment to one another with our community, where Leo cut the cupcakes with his sword cane, where we danced into the night and held each other tenderly.

About a year and a half later, Leo had transitioned toward a more masculine identity: top surgery, hormones, and changing their gender marker on their identity documents to M. Shanna's chronic pain and illnesses had become more intense, leading to relatively frequent ER trips, and they were traveling to Mississippi for a development training to support their work with a local reproductive justice organization. They were worried about ending up in the ER, offering their insurance card, and having to explain about domestic partner benefits (which is how they were covered through Leo's employer-sponsored health insurance) in a region that did not recognize them. We realized that even though civil unions and "same-sex" marriage were not legal, we as trans folks could game the system and still access legal protections due to the F and M on our driver's licenses.

On a random day in February 2013, we went to the county courthouse and clerk's office, first to register Shanna's car in the county we moved to, and then to head down the hall to get married. It almost didn't happen, as the electronic paperwork was pink (for Shanna) and blue (for Leo) and could not be switched. Shanna has had a lifelong aversion to pink as a stand-in for womanness/femininity/femmeness, as well as being incredibly stubborn, so you can imagine the conversation that ensued. However, Leo talked them down, a skill he remains so good at. Despite the clerk's confusion at us casually asking her to witness our marriage (in Colorado, you can self-solemnize your marriage), we were married standing at her desk and went to Saigon Basil, our favorite local Vietnamese place, for lunch to celebrate before heading back to work. Legal marriage felt like more of a means to an end (accessing rights, especially around health care) than a milestone in our relationship.

In the years that followed, Shanna started and finished their PhD, Leo's career took off, and eventually we moved to Michigan for Shanna's tenure-track job at a top-ranked university. There were ups and downs, especially as we mourned the loss of our community, navigated the shifts in Leo's career (he wound up starting his own PhD program in 2019), and discovered the beauty of a Michigan fall and the benefits of living so close to an airport in a place with a lower cost of living. We have always been nonmonogamous in identity, though not always in practice, and our move allowed us to explore new partners in a way we had not done in years. There were lots of feelings and lots of therapy, yet we had (and have) such unconditional positive regard for one another. Things were going . . . okay . . . for us, and then the pandemic hit.

Shanna

After well over a decade of living together, in December 2020 Leo told me he wanted to move out. I felt as though my heart cracked in two. We'd been together for a dozen years, and through multiple cross-state moves we had survived seven surgeries, a myriad of new diagnoses and mental health crises, my PhD program, the start of Leo's PhD program, new partners coming and going and coming and staying, and the first year of a life-altering pandemic. How could this be the moment when we were breaking up? And worse yet, I didn't understand why. He'd already been living and working in his own room for months, and he had his own space. What was it about me that he felt he needed to run from, especially after all this time? I was so hurt and unmoored in this moment, and I felt as though I was losing one of the loves of my life.

Leo

Of course, a decision like this does not come lightly nor without an immense amount of self-reflection. While I cannot speak on behalf of Shanna, it felt to me as if our relationship had gotten stuck in a cycle where neither of us felt good about it, despite us both working incredibly hard on ourselves and our relationship. We argued a lot, we disagreed a lot, and we cried a lot. For me, there was a lot of longing and grasping for what was. It felt as if we were trying to maintain homoeostasis in a space (literal and figurative) that no longer served us, rather than adapt and transform to a newer equilibrium where we both could thrive as individuals and as a couple. However, the hardest part was the unknown and wondering if that thriving could even occur.

We kept reminding each other that despite this loss, we'd always be family and in each others' lives. Interestingly enough, as soon as we moved through the major first set of emotions (OMG SO MUCH CRYING FROM EVERYONE) and started to think about how to divvy up our life together, something shifted. We realized we still loved each other, AND that our relationship (and with it, our proximity to one another) needed to shift. Maybe Leo could move out AND we could still be together, because, truly, what is more queer than saying no to enforced binaries ("you live together and are together," or "you live separately and are separate") and relationship ideals that simply did not serve us? As we discussed who would continue to cohabit with our cats (Shanna, with frequent visitation by Leo) and who would get the fancy new FireTV (Leo, one of the few things he really wanted), and divvied up the dishes, we also joked about queerly uncoupling, a nod to and a parody of Gwyneth Paltrow and Chris Martin's popularization of the term "consciously uncoupling."

Trying to explain this to our predominantly cisgender, heterosexual, monogamous family was an adventure. Our queer and polyamorous culture doesn't have a lot of role models or media examples to look to. How do you explain to folks who already weren't sure about queer and trans stuff, and who found our polyamory even harder to understand, that one of us was moving out and getting their own place but that we weren't actually breaking up? We got a lot of head nods and people saying "right," but we could already feel some of Leo's family pulling away. In our minds, it felt like they were putting Shanna in the "ex" column, even when we tried to explain that that wasn't the case. In the middle of all of this reframing and figuring out how to talk about and navigate all of this, Leo moved out.

Shanna

Even with almost a whole month to prepare, Leo's leaving was hard. Though he'd had his own room already for a while, we still usually ate together, slept together, and spent a lot of time together. Suddenly the house felt much emptier. Moreover, Leo's new apartment was hip and trendy, a flat above the main street in our college town. While that met his needs and desires in the moment perfectly, it also meant I got to see him a lot less. Two-hour parking limits meant no overnights at his place, and his decision to get a place up a flight of stairs—combined with me being disabled and very rarely able to navigate stairs, and even then with significant pain—felt like a clear boundary telling me I was not welcome there and that he would come to me, connecting only on his terms.

A few weeks later, he adopted Marla Pooch, the best pittie in the whole world (on my advice, of course). This lovely addition to our family sadly meant even less time together. Leo could no longer come and stay over; who would take Marla down those stairs for walkies and potty time? Adventures together had to be shortened in order for him to be home to take care of Marla. Sadly, Marla and the cats didn't get along, so our time to connect and be together became limited. Conversely, Marla loved Leo's other partner and her animals, so his time with her increased. As polyam folks, we know not to compare, but it was hard to see her get so much time with Leo and for me to feel as though I was losing them completely.

During his eight months in that apartment, I saw him so rarely, and it did feel like we actually had broken up. This was amplified due to the pandemic; as an immunocompromised person who didn't get to see anyone else in person outside of my two partners, I had basically lost access to one of them. It felt incredibly isolating. I nursed my hurt, processed in therapy and with ice cream, and a few months later, my other partner, Allie, moved in with me.

Leo

There was and continues to be a grieving process around this transformation of what was to what is. Perhaps it is all the societal and cultural messages and pressure we receive about how our lives are supposed to look and the paths we're supposed to take. But then again, Shanna and I never really wanted or desired more cishetero traditions or life paths. Nonetheless, we made a big shift, and changes are hard, especially for two neurodivergent folks. And we were both heartbroken and grieving the loss of the life we had planned as we began to explore the uncharted territory of the next iteration of us.

I got one of the only apartments I could find that was affordable, in the same area, and that had landlords with a decent reputation. Shifting from being a homeowner to a renter was also a really hard transition for me, but that's a whole other story. Unfortunately, this apartment was not accessible for Shanna, which really limited our time together. Honestly, those first eight months are just a blur in my memory, probably because I spent so much time intellectualizing my feelings of grief, loss, and being in constant transition.

The next biggest shift for us was Leo buying a ranch-style home in fall of 2021. Although there are a few steps to enter the home, there is a railing, and everything is on one level. Now Shanna could come visit him (and Marla!), and the relationship shifted back toward what we had originally hoped for—more texting and FaceTiming throughout the week, and an overnight at Leo and Marla's on a weekly basis. Leo's home even became a hospice for older and grumpy cats. Kinsey and Sir Catrick Stewart made their way to Leo's for their final days, valuing the routine and minimalism evident there. Allie and Shanna had their 2022 commitment ceremony rehearsal dinner in Leo's backyard, and Leo was in the ceremony, representing connection between both of Shanna's partners, and representing the polycule. Neither of us could have imagined this is how it would have worked out, but here we are, queering uncoupling, and figuring out how to recouple.

Shanna

Leo buying a single-story home felt like a really big deal for me. Yes, the few stairs can be a trip (literally), yet the intentionality of him choosing a place where I could visit helped rekindle our connection. I felt seen and heard and validated. There was a place for me to keep my ice packs and heating pads and meds, and a cube for my clothes. My intensely minimalist partner made space for me, literally and figuratively. In the past two and a half years, I have spent the night there approximately once a week, and usually Leo drops by Allie's and my place a few times a month for family dinner, or to see the cats, or for a fire pit. It feels like my family is back to being that—a family, even though we don't all live together, and even though Leo's and my relationship has changed. We are more romantic partners and best friends who know each other inside and out, and that is what works for us.

Leo's mom still sees me as her child-in-law, which is super meaningful to me, especially after recently losing my mother. My mother, who absolutely did not understand either polyamory or Leo moving out, loved both Leo and Allie so much, and my sister and her husband do as well. Our community gets it; almost everyone knows Leo and I live separately and that I live with Allie, and no one in my circles has assumed Leo and I don't love each other anymore (or at least no one has said so to my face). It feels like we've pulled it off, deconstructing and reconstructing systems to work for our love, our needs, and our desires. My home that I share with Allie is covered in artwork and tchotchkes and memories, and Leo's home is minimalist and zen. We are still together, *and* apart, our relationship having shifted to where it is today.

Leo

It was incredibly important to me to have a space that I could share with Shanna, and I am really glad that I have my own place that is true to me and provides the sanctuary I need to thrive. I call it my cozy cottage, but it is also a place where Shanna can be as well. Shortly after I moved into my house, I was talking on the phone with a former boss/current friend and updating her on all the things that had happened in the past year, and she said, "I totally get it. Shanna will always be your life partner." Honestly, that simple phrase helped me make sense of how I felt. Shanna is someone I always want to be in my life and vice versa. Cohabitating and legal documents don't make a family; as queers, we know this all too well. Shanna and I changed how the relationship looks on the outside, but that did not change how we felt about each other on the inside, and it absolutely did not erase the impact we'd had on each other in all the years prior. I think it is safe to say that we hold an immense amount of adoration, pride, and, of course, love for each other, and it is important to both of us to do the work to maintain those feelings, even when it can be hard, as things evolve and shift over time . . . just as life does.

And now, we are on our newest journey together: divorce! Yes, the big D word that everyone has been waiting for. However, just as our marriage was legal only and completed in isolation at the courthouse, so too will be our divorce. Leo is now a professor, making less money at a more community-focused institution, and it makes sense for him to not be married in order to have lower income-based student loan payments and to be in a lower tax bracket. Shanna hopes to legally marry Allie so they can access their health care benefits and more easily be "their person" in hospitals and other medical settings. So we have been struggling for months now, with our no-fault amicable divorce paperwork being rejected and denied, and we are currently waiting during the state-enforced separation waiting period (despite having lived and operated financially separately for over three years) so we can go to court and officially divorce. Then we hope that Allie and Shanna can get married before the US Supreme Court strikes Obergefell *down, limiting legal marriage for those with matching sex markers.*

We finally have court date set in a few months. Shanna, always the thespian, has planned out a whole story that ignores both of our transness (which feels like too much for the courts) and in which they play someone who has come out a lesbian, and Leo plays someone who has come out as a gay man. In this drama, we have realized we are both gay and have accidentally become each others' beards; therefore we must divorce in order to access our true selves, despite still loving each other. This involves outfits of buffalo plaid and leather boots for Shanna, and the gayest romper Leo can find. While Leo continues to remind Shanna that the judge won't even ask why we're divorcing, he is also playing along, as they always have, because we have consistently been a wonderful support team for each other: a loud and sassy femme, and a strong, amiable, put together transmasculine person, deeply in love, even as we divorce.

Epilogue

We finally divorced in April 2024, and we were about as visibly gay as you would expect, right down to Shanna donning a rainbow mask. As a foil to all the couples before us who were splitting up that day, with each person sitting alone at their own table on either side of the room, we opted to sit together, holding hands. The judge looked at us and did a double take as the case was read out loud. "You two look like you really care about each other," the judge said. "That's really nice to see." We smiled behind our masks and nodded. "You're sure you want to do this?" Again, we nodded, and just like that, we were divorced. It felt almost surreal. And just as Leo guessed, no one got to hear Shanna's whole screenplay of being queer for one another. The world (our local courthouse) has lost a performer indeed.

The timing couldn't have been better. A month or so later, Leo was offered his dream job in Colorado and has since moved back to Denver. This would have been infinitely more complicated if we were still legally connected. The move has been hard; more feelings, more tension, more complicated talks. Yet we remain family, continuing to connect as we are able, and even sharing a hotel room at a work conference, where we are writing this epilogue.

For a bunch of folks who don't believe in marriage, this is a lot of participating in government systems just to access rights and affordable health care, but here we are. We are queerly uncoupling and recoupling, queering love and relationships and government views of marriage; a perfect place for us to be as we create the world in which we wish to live.

Things I Lost in the Fire

JÁLYNN T. CASTLEMAN

If your house caught fire, what would you grab?

My mom talks about her experience of abuse like a frog being boiled in water. If you tried to drop a frog into boiling water, what would happen? She would jump right out. If you put a frog in a big, clean pot filled with cool water, she'll happily stay put. If you turn the burner on low, the bottom might get a little warm, but she probably wouldn't notice. She won't notice the temperature rising until it's too late.

My mom got engaged for the first time shortly after graduating from college. Young and lovestruck, she found the idea of being selected, of being chosen, to be intoxicating. It was easy to imagine riding that wave all the way to the altar. The water was warm and felt like home. It's hard to build something new on a foundation that feels like home, when home was never safe to begin with.

Her fiancé didn't slap her across the face the very first time another man looked at her. He didn't blacken her eye the first time she wore a pretty sundress and blushed at another man's attention. After all, she was his. Other men admiring her reflected well on him. Their appreciation validated his discerning taste. But he did beat her senseless when the praise became more about my mom as a person and less about his acquisition of her as another shiny plaything in his collection. Just as her mother had done to her.

Bloodied and bruised, my mom tried to understand what happened. His mother and aunt clicked their tongues at her while reviewing wedding plans: "Well, you've got to stop doing whatever it is that's making him angry. You brought this on yourself, you know."

He's too good for you. You're lucky to be getting married at all. Just be grateful someone wants you.

Years later, my mother found herself back in her snowy Midwestern hometown, a divorced single mom (divorced from a different man than her first fiancé; the abuse was subtler this time, because he had to keep up appearances, after all). Her new man—my father—was a charming, handsome, and very broke law student at the state university. Over the course of their twenty-year relationship, that broke law student became a not-so-broke lawyer at a white-shoe law firm in Manhattan. The abuse became subtler still, and somehow more painful.

That was my understanding of what a marriage should look like. Growing up, I watched my mother dim her light to keep from outshining my father. I learned that being a good wife meant slowly contorting myself to accommodate the needs of my partner so completely that, to paraphrase George Balanchine, if I was very lucky and I said my prayers, I would be blessed with a beautiful marriage.

But first, comes the sweat.

Beautiful marriages are earned, and your reward is only as sweet as your sacrifice.

What are you willing to give up to prove you are worthy?

You're so lucky to be getting married!

You're lucky to be getting married at all.

Honestly, you guys give me hope.

Just be grateful someone wants you.

That's how I ended up engaged, at twenty-five years old, to a woman ten years older than I was who couldn't bother to correct her family when they misspelled my name every single time they wrote it for the nine years we were together—in every text message, every card, even on the framed "guest book" from our wedding. I had found an idea on some wedding blog to take a photo from our engagement photoshoot and frame it with an oversized matboard.

The matboard served as the guestbook at our wedding where friends and family wrote us well wishes that I then hung on our living room wall. For over five years, I sat on the couch underneath an (unreasonably expensive) framed photo of us, wishing my ex and her new wife "Jaelyn," "Jaylynn"—or was it "Jaylin?"—a long life together.

My ex-wife did love me. She just didn't respect me. She told me all the time how much she loved me. Long, beautiful essays, artfully written cards, all of which ended up as evidence in our divorce hearing. She trained me to listen to her words and ignore her actions. It didn't matter if she stared at me blankly when I told her I was unhappy, or pretended like she didn't know me when we were out in public and ran into one of her mother's old friends from church.

I was trained to believe that none of that mattered. She took me on Caribbean vacations for my birthday, and everyone told me how beautiful our family was.

Our family was beautiful. Just like the family my mother had built for me. My mother poured herself into us, everything she had. We were her masterpiece. It felt disrespectful to love my own daughter any less fiercely than my own mother had loved me.

Why should it matter that the water around me was starting to simmer?

When I first took leave from work, I told my wife it was because I was overwhelmed. Overwhelmed by life, overwhelmed by the state of our marriage, overwhelmed by things at work, overwhelmed by everything.

When we went out to dinner for our fifth wedding anniversary, I tried to explain what was going on. I told her I felt like our marriage was a house that had caught fire, and I was trapped inside of it. "When we got married, it's like we built a house together," I explained. Over the course of those five years, life had kicked up all sorts of debris, dead leaves, and cigarette butts into our yard: difficulty conceiving, living through a global pandemic, navigating layoffs and job changes, losing loved ones unexpectedly. Is it any wonder the house our marriage built caught fire?

Once it started to burn, I looked to her for help. *Oh no!* I said. *Our house is burning. We really should do something.*

In response, she was silent. Our marriage house continued to burn.

After three years of saving and planning, and four rounds of fertility treatment (and countless tears, fights, and sleepless nights), we were blessed with a happy, healthy baby girl.

Our baby is finally here! I cried with relief. *But our house is still burning. Can't we do something to save it?*

She remained silent, unmoving, as if I hadn't spoken. Our marriage house continued to burn.

Two more years passed, and I felt like I was standing in that house, flames everywhere, clutching my baby to my chest, begging her to do something. By this point, the fire department had responded: Those closest to us had noticed our dysfunction. Like helicopters circling overhead, other friends began to gossip, murmuring among themselves like sympathetic reporters safely ensconced in their studio miles away, shaking their heads and commenting on the devastation as it unfolded.

After (yet another) round of couples' therapy that my ex quit midsession, and an unexpected surgery for our daughter, the exhaustion of carrying our family through all of that madness drove me to take medical leave from work.

Only then did my wife finally turn to me and say, *What's that smell? Is something burning?*

But it was too late.

The couple of years it took to navigate our divorce and custody proceedings were, simply put, hell on earth. More than once, I wondered if I'd made the right choice. I wondered if there would be anything left worth saving after the brimstone raining down on me destroyed any hope of a relationship (familial, platonic, or otherwise) between my ex-wife and me. I wondered what I would do after the hellfire of my ex's rage (read: embarrassment, shame, self-pity, internalized homophobia, and religious trauma) finished razing to the ground the life we had built together over the last decade.

In the depths of the perdition of our custody battle, I felt like I was living in one of those Lifetime movies my mom used to watch on Sunday afternoons while I was growing up.

Instead of working with me to find a responsible path toward separate households and coparenting, my ex-wife established an encampment in our dining room. She refused to move out and threatened to strip me of custody of our daughter if I even thought about leaving. For months, she slept on an air mattress (and later, a camping cot) behind the hastily hung curtain she used as a door, and she watched me.

She recorded my comings and goings from our apartment without my knowledge or consent. At one point in our custody battle, a video surfaced of her gleefully narrating my actions as she videotaped me taking our daughter to day care in the morning, speculating aloud about who was driving the car we were getting into. It was an Uber.

If I left the house in the evening after our toddler was asleep and my ex saw me, I'd get a nasty text the following morning, accusing me of shirking my responsibilities as a mother, leaving her to care for our daughter by herself all night. Our daughter was two at the time, attending full-day day care. Once she was down, that child slept like a rock for at least nine hours.

When I finally got up the courage to spend the night outside the marital residence, my ex-wife harassed me with relentless phone calls and text messages, demanding to know where I was. When I refused to tell her (reminding her that when it wasn't my night with our daughter, I was free to live my life as I pleased), she accused me of being an addict who was mentally unstable, an unfit mother who was drinking so much on weeknights she couldn't find her way home, and countless other figments of her troubled imagination.

In the hardest moments of my divorce, I finally understood why people stay. Why someone might choose to give in to the fire destroying their marriage, rather than stand up and fight. That's what my ex did. She succumbed to the smoke, quietly surrendering to living in a soulless marriage. Like her mother did. And her mother before her. She was taught to believe that marriages weren't living things to be nurtured. They were static, stable. Stoic.

To her, I had committed the ultimate sin: I tried to leave our marriage house. When my need for more than the stoic shell she'd built around us became so great that the house caught fire, my punishment was to burn along with it.

After almost a year of living under the same roof, surviving the emotional and psychological abuse my ex-wife subjected me to, the judge assigned to our case had finally had enough. By judicial order, I was granted the right to move out of the marital residence and move on with the rest of my life.

When I left that house, I left so much behind: memories, attachments, hopes of what I'd imagined for our future, my identity as a wife and mother. Like discarded baggage, I left all of it behind, along with my keys and laundry card, when I shut the door for the last time. Nearly five years earlier, I had entered the space as a young wife and new mother, full of optimism and hope for the beautiful marriage and family we were going to build. When I left for the last time, I was a divorced single mom with more debt than I'd ever had in my life, and the conviction of someone who'd walked through fire and lived to tell the tale. That fire destroyed everything in its wake and cleared space for new growth.

If you ask any plant person, they'll tell you that growing something new takes time, patience, and more than a little bit of luck. Instead of using the same blueprint to create another foundation, I tried something new. Instead of building a house, I planted a garden.

The process isn't linear. It can take years for plants to grow and bear fruit, even in the best conditions. I wouldn't describe the years of my divorce and the immediate aftermath as the best of anything; and yet, during that time I was lucky enough to see some of the seeds I planted start to sprout. Green, vibrant, alive.

Working with nature, rather than against it, is messy and unpredictable. Some days it's more overwhelming than I have the capacity to hold. Other days are unexpectedly glorious, and I can start to see what a new future could look like. Even on the toughest days, I know I'm creating something worthwhile. Something healthy. Something my daughter will recognize in others and will know is safe to build upon because it's warm and feels like home.

The Pregnant Predicament

THOMAS BEATIE

I deeply loved Nancy, who is now my ex-wife. For fourteen years, she was my loyal companion as we navigated life and countless exciting adventures. Our journey was a complex tapestry woven from dreams, struggles, and shared aspirations. It was as if we were characters in a story we wrote together, each chapter filled with vivid moments and challenges that tested the strength of our love and the depths of our resilience.

Our union was more than just a romantic entanglement; it was a deliberate act of defiance against the rigid societal norms that sought to define us. Like many, we shared a dream of fighting for happiness in a world that seemed to sparingly grant that universal privilege. The forefathers of our nation recognized that happiness is a fundamental pursuit for all people, as expressed in the US Declaration of Independence, which asserts the right to "life, liberty, and the pursuit of happiness." My sixth great-grandfather, Benjamin Harrison, was a signer of this founding document, which established the principles that would guide the nation's government and identity. Fittingly, as his blood runs through my veins, I found myself carrying on his legacy in my own pursuit of happiness and the identity that accompanied it.

Some people say a marriage certificate is just a piece of paper; just live your life and be happy. However, the right to marry is about far more than the title or the ceremony. It represents access to essential legal protections, social equality, and personal dignity. I wanted to marry my fiancée, but at the time, the government said I couldn't. A single letter (F vs. M) made all the difference in whether I could marry the person I loved.

Nancy and I were passionate in the fight for marriage equality for everyone. We were deeply committed to the cause, recognizing the stark inequalities that same-sex couples faced in accessing the legal rights and benefits freely available to different-sex couples. Together, we lobbied legislators, testified at Senate hearings, and organized protests, all in the name of advocating for the rights of same-sex couples to marry. As part of a larger movement, Nancy and I were instrumental in the passage of Hawaii's hate crimes law in 2001. This legislation was the state's first to include protections for gays and lesbians, and it was eventually amended to include transgender individuals as well. In that same year, we helped organize the March for Equality, a grueling seven-day, 110-mile march around the island of Oahu, symbolizing our relentless struggle for equal rights. This march reached its crescendo with a symbolic commitment ceremony on the steps of the state capitol, where Nancy and I, along with other couples, declared our unwavering commitment to each other. Despite the significant opposition and challenges we faced, our activism was fueled by a deeply personal desire for equal recognition and rights as a couple.

All my life, I had embodied a masculine energy. As a child, I was a visible tomboy. I didn't just admire Superman; I wanted to be Superman. This male-centric identity never waned. Before I started a romantic relationship with Nancy in 1998, I already looked and carried myself like a man. Like billions of people, I was a person with a male gender identity who was attracted to women.

The government had a process for changing one's legal gender, and I followed it. I began testosterone therapy, underwent surgery, and officially updated my name and sex marker on my state and federal documents, including my driver's license, birth certificate, passport, and Social Security index. With that simple change to the letter "M," I would finally be able to legally marry Nancy. And yet, I was still the same person—just with a change of a single letter. This seemingly small alteration in identity would carry monumental significance, shifting the world's perception while leaving the core of who I was untouched.

Nancy and I were married in Hawaii on February 5, 2003. We went to a government building in downtown Honolulu for our ceremony. The setting was simple: a justice of the peace's office, adorned only with a single white rose and a vine-themed backdrop. Nancy and I were joined by her oldest daughter and her boyfriend, as well as one of our mutual friends, who served as our witness. As anticipated, none of my family showed up. I wore beige slacks and a periwinkle shirt, while Nancy looked stunning in a simple lavender dress that matched me. The ceremony, though small and intimate, was everything we had hoped for. It was a culmination of our struggles and triumphs, a testament to our love that transcended cultural barriers. We exchanged vows that felt like a promise to the universe itself—a promise of fidelity, partnership, and an unyielding pursuit of happiness. As we left the office, the reality of our union set in: We were now a family, recognized by the world, and ready to face whatever came our way, together.

We then started anew, relocating ourselves and my business, Define Normal—a custom screen-printing and retail clothing company I had started in 1997—from Hawaii to central Oregon. The move was symbolic, a chance to escape the echoes of our past and the judgments of those who couldn't understand our journey. In Oregon, we planted the seeds of a new life. We purchased a beautiful home in a charming neighborhood, two rental properties, and half an acre on a bluff in a desirable central part of the city, where undeveloped lots were beginning to give way to custom homes overlooking the skyline—the place where we planned to build our dream home. Financially, we were set, but there lingered a void that whispered of something missing; a dream unrealized, a future not yet fulfilled.

In 2006, I embarked on the journey of pursuing my vision of starting a family—a path filled with uncertainty but anchored by a deep desire for parenthood. Nancy was wholeheartedly supportive of this dream of raising a child together. We faced crucial questions: Would we adopt? Would we use a surrogate? Or would I be the one to bear our child? These were not decisions we took lightly.

Surrogacy and adoption, while valuable options for many, presented complexities that we were not ready to navigate. The legal intricacies, emotional uncertainties, and financial burdens were daunting enough, yet they were not the core of my hesitation. The thought of entrusting another with the intimate process of nurturing our child before birth weighed heavily on me. Nancy, twelve years my senior, had undergone a hysterectomy two decades earlier due to severe endometriosis. Meanwhile, I had made the deliberate choice to retain my reproductive organs, driven by a desire to one day become a father and to have my own biological children—perhaps even grandchildren—to carry on the family legacy.

Retaining my reproductive ability did not detract from my male identity; in fact, it reinforced it. I had never envisioned the possibility of pregnancy for myself, but sterilization was never on the table. I always believed I would find a way when the time came. Ultimately, I came to the realization that I was the best choice to be the one to provide the environment, the nourishment, and the care that only I could ensure. If neither Nancy nor I could have become pregnant, we would have considered surrogacy or adoption, but not to conform to cultural demands or to make others feel comfortable. While our choices were unorthodox, they were also deeply personal, guided by the desire to create a family on our own terms.

Eventually the day arrived. After a year and a half of rejections and discrimination from fertility doctors, clinic psychologists, and ethics boards, we finally found a doctor willing to help us access a cryobank, and I became pregnant. As the baby grew within me, my concerns about the legal protections for our family also grew. Seeking guidance, I contacted an LGBT publication, asking what others in my position had done. They invited me to write a first-person article, where I said that "our situation sparks legal, political, and social unknowns." This was a moment, not just for us but also for the broader society grappling with the evolving definitions of family and identity. What I eventually realized was that, legally, this was unprecedented. There was no road map for our situation, not even an online support group. We were navigating waters not only for ourselves but also for others who might follow in our footsteps.

How would I be classified on my baby's birth certificate if I brought any attention to myself? Would this mean I'd have to give birth in secret at home?

After all, my goal was to blend into the world. Would our marriage be challenged? My own father, who was unsupportive and called our marriage a sham, was a threat. Would he take our child and my estate? These questions loomed large, casting darkness over our joy. I wanted to ensure that if something happened to me, Nancy would be our child's legal mother and guardian. On a deeply personal level, I wanted to preserve my legal identity as husband, father, and man.

Unexpectedly, the media's interest hit a flashpoint, as if a match had been struck in a room filled with kindling. The small piece I had written, hidden on page 24 of the magazine, was a bid to seek understanding and support. It was intended to be a personal narrative, a glimpse of the unique journey Nancy and I had embarked upon together. However, the world had other plans.

Within days of the article's publication, the story of "the pregnant man" exploded across the media landscape. Major networks, newspapers, and websites around the globe picked up the story, each one eager to dissect and discuss the implications of my pregnancy. The story crossed borders and languages, appearing in headlines from New York to Tokyo, captivating audiences with its out-of-the-ordinary nature. Paparazzi, especially from the UK and Germany, descended upon our once-quiet neighborhood, their cameras ready to capture any glimpse of the man carrying a child. At the time, the public knew little to nothing about the existence of transgender men. The idea that these types of men might want to reproduce was even more far-flung. Nevertheless, the story of a transgender person giving birth was not the focus. The imagery fascinated the media, intensified by the fact that I was legally and fully documented as male. Our lives, previously defined by a sense of privacy and normalcy, were thrust into the glaring spotlight of public scrutiny.

Since childhood, my two greatest fears have always been public speaking and getting eaten by a shark (in that order). Yet with all of the wild rumors and bizarre tales being spun about our story—like how my penis would explode during labor or that I might give birth to kittens—I felt obligated to set the record straight. Rather than let the tabloids conjure things up and control the narrative, I agreed to speak with what I considered to be the most reputable and respected source reaching out to me: Oprah Winfrey. Surely this would be the best way to have a larger and more mature dialogue about acceptance and the limitless possibilities of self-agency.

On her TV show, she asked me if I felt conflicted about being a man and doing something that men don't typically do, like giving birth. I said, "I have a very stable male gender identity. I see pregnancy as a process, and it doesn't define who I am. . . . It's not a male or female desire to want to have a child. It's a human desire. I'm a person, and I have the right to have my own biological child." Oprah replied, "Yes, you do have that right."

While some celebrated our courage and saw our story as a beacon of progress, most others met it with skepticism and disdain. By my lowball calculations, over 99.99 percent of online comments were unsupportive. It was surreal to see celebrities I once admired not only mentioning my name but mocking me. The Fox network had commentators predicting that I'd give birth to a three-eyed Ewok and literally said I should kill myself. There were organizations in existence to help protect lesbian, gay, bisexual, and transgender people against defamation in the media, yet those guardians were invisible. I felt like I had no one supporting me—not even the historically discriminated-against community that I was a part of and fought for. Heads from most of the national LGBT organizations reached out to me in a conference call before my Oprah appearance to urge me not to do the show. They were concerned that my message would undermine the community in some way and that the world was not ready for this. When I did not comply with their directives or accept their talking points, they effectively ostracized me from the community. Other people within transgender circles called me a maverick and said I had gone rogue by deviating from the collective trans script at the time, which held that I was supposed to feel so much discomfort with my own body that I should never want to use it to procreate. It was widely expected that if one were to choose to transition to the opposite sex, one should also consent to giving up the right to reproduce. I wholeheartedly disagreed with this view. I didn't feel like I was born in the wrong body. I was born exactly the way I was meant to be: myself. Sterilization wasn't going to make me any more or less of either sex; it would only make me sterile, stripping me of the privilege of being a biological parent.

Then started a concerted effort to try to deflect my story and tamp it down by asserting that I was not the first transgender person to give birth. In fact, I assumed I was likely not; the notion of being transgender doesn't have to be proved through modifying one's body or official documents. This was not a contest, a very unpopular one at that, for bragging rights. However, my situation was different—one of navigating the framework of my legal male identity and preserving the rights of my family in a way no one else had been tested, securing protections for those who followed. I was saddened and frustrated by the LGBT community. If any population should know better, how was it that we were still battling among ourselves for basic rights and liberties within our own diverse community? Despite being told I should be silent and cower in the shadows—as if I could hide my belly—I felt that there was clearly a need for my voice to be heard.

The polarized reactions were a reminder to me of the work that still lay ahead, not just for us but for anyone daring to live authentically in the face of social pressures. I tried not to take it to heart when people accused me of having a baby just to create a publicity stunt and said I was only visible to become rich and famous. Though a rumor started that we were paid $1 million to appear on Oprah's show, Nancy and I were compensated with nothing but a few promotional items bearing her name: a T-shirt, a mug, and a hat. Oprah saw us as a human-interest story, and we knew that our story was bigger than us. It was part of a greater conversation that needed to be had about protection of identity and reproductive freedom. The media's gaze, intense and unrelenting, was a force we could not control, but it was also an opportunity. As the media attention continued, we learned to navigate this new reality, balancing the public's curiosity with our desire for privacy. We became adept at sharing our story on our terms, ensuring that the narrative reflected the love and hope that defined our journey.

Due to our widely discussed story, the Oregon state registrar was alerted to my impending delivery. Now it was the government's turn to push back. Suddenly, that "M" was not as permanent as I had thought. They had no formalized policy on how to treat my situation—a person with male credentials giving birth. Even my health insurance and hospital band read "male." Initially, they listed Nancy as "father" and me as "mother" on our daughter Susan's birth certificate. I found ironic humor in how easily they allowed Nancy to be classified as a man when she identifies as a woman, especially after all the extensive processes I had to go through to fight for my identity. Realizing their error, they revised it, issuing a "parent/parent" classification internally coded for same-sex female partners, which didn't reflect us.

Hoping to easily resolve this issue, I requested a copy of my own birth certificate from Hawaii to provide to Oregon Vital Records. I was shocked to discover that someone pretending to be me had mailed in a request to Hawaii's Vital Records office, asking to change my birth certificate to female. The people I spoke to in Hawaii assured me that they'd flagged the request as suspicious and that they'd taken no action because they were aware of my visibility. Nevertheless, it was a poignant illustration that other people wanted to control the structure of our family and how we chose to live our lives. What could motivate an anonymous person to take such actions? It was scary and unnerving to know that I had both visible and invisible forces working against me to try to undermine my peace.

Ultimately, both Nancy and I had to adopt Susan as mother and father to ensure her birth certificate was correct. We repeated this process for her brothers, Austin and Jensen, borne by me in succeeding years. Creating our now-sizable family was a long, hard battle, but by 2010, it felt like we had achieved the American dream. Our home was filled with the laughter of children, the walls adorned with memories of our shared adventures, each picture a testament to our resilience and love. Life seemed poised for smooth sailing—until it wasn't.

My "Define Normal" warehouse and showroom that I had once opened to the public was now closed to walk-ins. Due to roving reporters, paparazzi, and the intermittent death threats my family and I had been receiving, I no longer felt safe letting just anyone be around us. My business suffered because of it. Then, in the first week of May 2010, there was a flash crash in the stock market, and the Dow Jones Industrial Average dropped over a thousand points within minutes. Both Nancy and I had brokerage accounts with various stocks and positions that reacted to the turbulence, and they sharply declined as well. Before the value of the stocks rebounded, the brokerage house sold our positions on margin at the worst possible prices, causing the value of our accounts—which had been worth over $800,000—to essentially become worthless. To make matters worse, four of our five properties were now underwater on their mortgages due to the housing bubble caused by the global financial crisis. We would not be able to continue paying our mortgages with the loss of our savings. All four of our properties in Oregon went into foreclosure. Nancy and I packed us all up, three babies included, in a U-Haul with our remaining belongings and made the long trek from Oregon to Arizona, to live in our only remaining property. Our goal was to overcome the financial wrecking ball we had endured and hopefully rebuild our lives using the same strength of sinew that had held us together for so long.

Like undoubtedly everyone, I did not get married expecting to also get divorced. My parents were married until death did they part. For me, marriage represented a lifelong commitment. I believed I had won the relationship lottery—and Nancy with me—in finding the right person to spend the rest of our lives with. This is why I was devastated when I realized I had to file for divorce. Everyone's love story plays out differently, and ours was cut short due to a lack of self-awareness, an inability to change for the better, and a waning passion to endure. People and circumstances change. Nancy had turned to self-medicating. Along with our financial woes, Nancy was fighting demons while dealing with a recent discovery that the man she'd been led to believe was her biological father all her life was not really her biological father. Her actual biological father lived in Arizona, and he was the reason why we had bought a home there. Now he had turned his back on her as she continued to fall deeper into her addictions. At the same time, her wealthy mother tragically died in a car accident, and Nancy discovered that she'd been cut out of her mother's will. Nancy fell deeper and deeper into self-sabotage that affected everyone around her. I held on for as long as I could, but the bond, respect, and trust that had once defined my relationship with her had become irrevocably fractured. While I didn't want to be a quitter—I had vowed to stick it out in good times and bad—becoming a parent shifted my priorities. My children's safety and welfare became my top concern. Ultimately, I felt that leaving Nancy and fighting for sole custody was in everyone's best interest.

In early 2012, I moved into a two-bedroom apartment. I then filed an order of protection for my children and myself against Nancy, along with legal separation paperwork that later transitioned into divorce proceedings. Some of the more egregious reasons for my actions included being awakened at 2:00 a.m. one morning by her punching me in the face; another time, she forcefully rolled a stroller into my genitals after I had just undergone lower surgery. Most indelibly marked in my mind was a time when she was passed out on the floor, intoxicated. Food was burning on the stove as our babies climbed on her insensate body.

In response to the documents served upon her, Nancy lashed out with anger and desperation. She took possession of our only car by snatching the keys against my will. She emptied the contents of our safe, including my family's heirloom jewelry and my coin collection. She also swiped my business debit card, visiting ATM after ATM until the cash was depleted, using up the money intended to pay the bills and mortgage and causing the account to run deeply negative on overdraft protection. The bank let her get away with it unpunished. They viewed her actions as a dispute between married spouses, even though I owned the business before we were together and she wasn't on the account.

The divorce courtroom became a battleground, echoing with the clashing narratives of our once-unified life. Her attorney attempted to depict me as unloving toward my own children, a controlling and violent person, and particularly blamed my testosterone prescription as the reason, along with my capabilities as a black belt in tae kwon do. He was intent on dismissing Nancy's aggression and emphasizing the stereotype that only women are the victims of domestic violence—and that the best place for children is with their mother. My lawyer focused on the danger the children were in due to her addiction and the poor choices she made while they were under her care.

An Arizona Superior Court judge temporarily granted me sole custody while ordering Nancy to participate in the drug court system. I was also required to pay spousal support. However, during the process, the judge admitted that he had read a Yahoo.com article about me giving birth. This disclosure marked a turning point in his demeanor and rulings. He questioned my legal male identity and the legitimacy of our marriage, citing the fact that same-sex marriage was illegal at the time in both Arizona and Hawaii. Seemingly out of spite, he made comments that he did not have a problem taking the children from me and awarding sole custody to Nancy. He refused to consider gender identity, hormone treatment, and sex-change surgery as grounds for successful gender transition. In his ruling, he said that if the court were to agree that a man can give birth, such a precedent "would lead to circumstances in which a person's sex can become a matter of whim and not a matter of any reasonable, objective standard or policy, which is precisely the kind of absurd result the law abhors." He said he could find no definition of a man as someone who can give birth. I thought it was unexpectedly emasculating of him that he saw a man as someone who can't do something.

The truth is that it would have been easier and more beneficial for me to claim that we weren't legally married. For a moment in time, Nancy, too, was going to fight our marriage's legality, and she deadnamed me and referred to me with female pronouns until she realized that she would not receive any spousal support. Even though we were now on opposite sides, this posture wounded me deeply—that she'd choose to destroy what I thought we both believed in. I could have believed this about anyone else in the world, except her.

We ended up selling the house, even though she tried to fight that too. Neither of us had enough money to support ourselves. Despite the judge invalidating our marriage, I started selling our possessions at garage sales and online auctions, splitting the money equally with her. The irony is that if I had not worried about Nancy's parental rights and had not doubled down on ensuring them by allowing her to adopt our children, this judge would have been obligated to let me have my children without a fight. Yet, the validating of our marriage, along with the double-edged sword of rights, was exactly what I wanted. Many people had told me to be careful what I wished for, but I still regretted nothing.

The judge paused my spousal support obligations but ruled that Arizona had no jurisdiction over the divorce, stating we needed to resolve it in Hawaii, where the union took place. That would have required all of us, including the children, to be uprooted and move back to Hawaii, a place I had already successfully escaped. We'd have to live there for six months to regain residency before filing for divorce and then endure the full term of the divorce proceedings. This was not only impractical but also unaffordable, especially since our divorce should have been granted in Arizona like anyone else's. Furthermore, the judge abruptly allowed Nancy to exit the drug court system without completing it, then granted her joint custody of the children, nullifying the remainder of the order of protection. After nine months of only strict and supervised visits, the children, ages two, three, and four, found themselves thrust into unfamiliar surroundings for half of every week.

When Nancy and I lived together, Child Protective Services assigned me as the only safety monitor for our children. She was never allowed to be left alone with them. Yet, now that we lived apart, there was nobody to protect them from her. My children had become my reason and meaning in life. And here my worst fears came true: I was no longer able to ensure their safety and welfare. I was beside myself, and my world felt like it was moving out from under me. When Nancy threatened to disappear to California with our children, I felt helpless and desperate. I couldn't sleep at night, fearing that their lives would be put in danger. Not wanting to tempt fate, I did something I thought would protect them. I placed a GPS tracking device on our family car. It was the only peace of mind I had about where they were when she had them.

In another court during the same window of time, Nancy was found guilty of violating the order of protection I had against her. She had harassed me with more than fifty text messages and calls per day, and she physically attacked me in a park at a child exchange by twisting and scratching my arm. In *State v. Nancy Beatie*, she received a misdemeanor for domestic violence. The judge asked if I would like to press charges. I declined, because while I was concerned about her actions, I did not want her life to be negatively affected by punitive sanctions, especially ones that might have affected her ability to provide for herself or the children. She was sentenced to pay a $300 fine and attend domestic violence classes. As we were walking out of the courthouse after her trial, Nancy was visibly angry. She began to follow me and verbally taunt me, vowing to get me thrown in jail. I turned the corner and walked directly into the room designated for filing orders of protection, and I renewed my order for another year.

I don't have many fond memories from this period in my life. Much of what I had fought for and built was shattered, leaving me in a fog where it was hard to envision a bright future. Then, unexpectedly, my luck began to change. The Cantor Law Group came to my aid, offering crucial pro bono support to combat the blatant injustice I faced from Arizona's Superior Court. The Transgender Law Center also stepped up by filing an amicus brief that advocated for both mine and Nancy's interests, aiming to validate our marriage and facilitate a resolution through divorce. Despite the best efforts of these legal experts to find any precedents relevant to my situation, there was no existing case law to reference a man or husband giving birth. Consequently, this matter of first impression was brought before the Arizona Court of Appeals.

Finally, the big day arrived regarding the appellate court's decision that would affect the fate of my family. I was cautiously optimistic but still traumatized from previous disappointments. Lo and behold, the tide had changed. The appellate judges stunningly ruled in my favor on August 13, 2014, affirming that I had properly updated my birth certificate and other legal documents to reflect my male gender under Hawaii law. They recognized the integrity of my identity and the legality of my marriage, providing a semblance of validation in a world that often casts doubt on my existence. They also noted that Arizona's gender marker requirements were similar to Hawaii's but less stringent, meaning our marriage would have been valid in Arizona as well. The court cited the Full Faith and Credit Clause of the Constitution, requiring Arizona to recognize our marriage. The appellate court reversed the lower court's decision, rejecting the notion that I was female because I had given birth, affirming my legal identity as a man, and recognizing our marriage.

This landmark case was more than just a divorce. It clarified that transgender people don't need to sterilize themselves to live authentic lives. The case started off as *Beatie v. Beatie*, but it evolved into the state of Arizona versus transgender people, human reproductive rights, and fairness under the law. This ruling came at a pivotal moment, not just for me but for the broader conversation about transgender rights. Had it been issued after June 26, 2015—when same-sex marriage became legal nationwide—my case might have been moot, as both opposite-sex and same-sex marriages would have been equally valid. This decision was a triumph for transgender reproductive rights, marking the first time a court recognized that men could give birth. It was a beacon of hope for transgender men worldwide now exploring parenthood, a promise that their rights and identities could be upheld. The underdog had finally prevailed. A weight felt like it was literally lifted from my body. I could once again imagine a future, vivid with possibilities. However, while it was liberating that Nancy and I had won the right to officially get a divorce, we still needed to go back to court to finalize it.

Divorce court, sadly, was not the kind of court that would soon be calling my name. There ended up being an issue with me putting a GPS tracker on the family car. The car was, in fact, registered in only my name, yet I still had to walk or ride a bike to get to work because I was without it. While Arizona is a community property state, the original divorce court judge had temporarily nullified our marriage, which should have even more strongly proved my ownership. Not only did I have a vested interest in the location of my property, but it was also perfectly legal to track your own minor children.

Nancy didn't see things the same way. When the device was discovered, she reported it to authorities and pressed charges. Of course, the picture she painted was that I was dangerous and jealous, and I wanted her back—all the opposite of the truth. I only wanted to avoid her. When the police showed up unannounced, I was the manager of a health food store, unsuspectingly standing behind the cash register. My employees lingered in disbelief as I was handcuffed and marched out the door.

On November 20, 2014, I was hauled to the jail in downtown Phoenix, booked, fingerprinted, and charged with felony stalking—fear for safety. Prior to this, I hadn't even received a parking ticket. My mugshot was taken, which quickly materialized on TMZ's website and across the media.

Once in custody, the correctional officers demanded to know if I had a penis and asked me to take down my pants. They said they needed to know if they should put me with the men or the women. I felt violated and refused to show them my privates. I told them that I had had surgery and had a penis. "I'm a man and want to be put with the men," I exclaimed. I understood that there was a greater chance of me being harmed by the men, but I was not going to compromise my identity and dignity. Luckily, I did not have to endure being strip-searched. They threw me into a holding cell with about a dozen unsavory-looking guys. I pleaded not guilty and was released the next day after seeing a judge for my initial appearance.

The detective and state prosecutor trying my case didn't want me to go unpunished; since I was a high-profile person, they wanted to make an example of me. Unsurprisingly, Nancy wanted them to throw the book at me. I was given a public defender and continued to press for my innocence. I knew what I had done was not out of malice toward Nancy; it was only to protect the well-being of my children. Yet who would be chosen to be on the grand jury? Would they be swayed to dislike me and side against me because of who I am, just like the majority of the general public, who couldn't understand my unusual story? How could I trust the legal system when the divorce court judge used his own personal bias against me? I was told the statistic about how state prosecutors have a 95 percent chance of winning their cases. A felony conviction could deliver serious consequences to my life, affecting my ability to find a new job, rent or buy a home, vote, and even keep my children. The state was offering me a plea deal, reducing my felony charge to a misdemeanor of disorderly conduct. Though I felt that I had a chance of winning due to the facts of my case and the intent of my motivation, any risk of losing my children was way too great. I took the plea bargain. Nancy told the judge that she was afraid for her life, asserted I'd leave the country with the kids, and pressed for three years of supervised probation. I was given a fine of $65 per month and twelve months of unsupervised probation, which was later reduced to six months due to good behavior.

Though the consequences of my misdemeanor were relatively lenient, it still affected my ability to get gainful employment and required me to pass extra security protocols to enter my daughter's school grounds. The worst of the damage was done to my public persona and reputation. While being a pregnant man was not a popular label, now being seen as a "Lifetime movie stalker" on top of it surely didn't help. On the contrary, Nancy's misdemeanor never affected her. She had purposely given the court an incorrect birthdate and Social Security number so that the charge would not stick to her record. Until this day, the court is still none the wiser, and the negative fallout from having a record has left her unscathed.

Divorce is inherently a challenging and complex process, fraught with emotional, legal, and financial difficulties. The legal complications of being a transgender man who had given birth to his own children, all while navigating a bitter divorce intertwined with criminal court proceedings, proved to be interminable, grueling, and soul scouring. A typical uncontested divorce in Arizona takes ninety to 120 days, with expedited cases taking around sixty days. Mine took over three and a half years, each day a reminder of the complexities and prejudices embedded in the legal system. On September 21, 2015, my divorce was finalized. However, it wasn't until July 2, 2024—over twelve years after filing—that I was granted sole physical and legal custody of Susan, Austin, and Jensen. My children were finally set free to choose where they wanted to live.

My experiences as a transgender man over the last twenty-eight years—through engagement, marriage, family building, and divorce—have profoundly shaped me. I can honestly say that my ordeal of going through a divorce has been one of the toughest journeys of my life. I lived through my identity and legal recognition being invalidated; custody of my children and parental rights being challenged; judicial bias and discrimination, along with social stigma, affecting the fairness of my outcomes; financial vulnerabilities; limited resources and anemic support; time behind bars; and devastating emotional and psychological tolls. I've faced deep disappointments, particularly from people I thought I could trust: family members, friends, and the LGBT community. While it's heartbreaking, I've come to understand that anyone—even doctors, government officials, and judges—can be cruel and discriminatory, wielding their biases in ways that profoundly impact lives. In the face of such adversity, I've learned to stand my ground and to find strength in my identity and the journey that has brought me here. As we endure the second Trump administration, I fear that respect and basic rights for transgender people will face greater challenges. To this day, I still receive death threats. Yet I draw strength from the lessons I've learned: Be vigilant and aware as you persevere, and always fight for what you believe in. There are people who will lift you up, and true love does prevail. My experiences have taught me to learn from every relationship, especially the ones that fail.

It's an unusual twist of events that Nancy and I continued fighting for our marriage as we promised each other on our wedding day—albeit through divorce. Despite the horrendous rupture we endured, my sincere wish for Nancy is that she finds the inner peace and love she truly deserves. Although my past has left me deeply wounded, I still choose to believe in the possibilities that life offers. I have discovered new love and the strength to begin anew. Today, I live with Susan, Austin, and Jensen in Phoenix, Arizona, with my second wife, Amber, and our six-year-old son, Jackson, who was conceived not by me but by Amber through in vitro fertilization using frozen specimens from the same anonymous donor whose sperm I used for my other children. Coincidentally, the phoenix is also a mythical bird that symbolizes rising from the ashes with renewal. I have become a CFP® professional, and I work as a financial advisor at a prestigious investment firm, having learned to better protect my family's financial security. Amber has taught me to trust being vulnerable despite my past, and to be a better communicator within a relationship. I am also constantly in pursuit of self-discovery and improvement, learning the most important lessons from the wisest of teachers—my own children. My dream is to give them the best chance of success at realizing their full potential. For everyone in my life, my ultimate goal is to be the best dad, husband, and man that I can be. Each day, I am grateful for the life we have built, the small victories that accumulate into a life of meaning and purpose. Our home is a sanctuary, a place where love and acceptance are the unwavering foundations.

Above all, I have learned to be myself and hold fast to the time-tested values: life, liberty, and the pursuit of happiness.

Your Survival Is Not Guaranteed

LIZ HARDWICK

Sweet One.

Here is how you might get through. I write this knowing how preposterous it is for you to consider this right now. That you will survive is a tenuous thought. There is no tinder, the harsh wind is too much, the spark of this idea has no potential to grow into a full-blown flame. All that is clear to you is that some people don't survive divorce.

The bruising runs deep. Your body is stiff, nothing bends anymore. You are brittle from all the weeping. The truth is, you may not survive this. There are people haunted for the rest of their lives. Your friends tell you about their resentful mothers who led lonely, futile lives. You can't decide if they are telling you as a warning or a prediction. You don't have the energy to decide the answer.

This missive is not about silver linings. It's also not about warnings. You won't find instructions here. Now is not the time. There is only grim grinding through, and it is a miracle each morning that you wake up, that you breathe, that you find the will to move your body and to feed your kids.

When you finally begin to go out in public, people will grip your biceps at the doorway of the coffee shop. It feels similar to when you were eight months pregnant, with the outpouring of birth stories from minor acquaintances. Now, the people who have a divorce under their belts take hold of your arm and say, "You will get through it. My life is better now." They offer assurances that you will become more whole.

"You have to let everything burn down," they say. "You are going through a portal." The phoenix metaphor will get tossed at you. You will contemplate the great red bird, soaring wide wings. The flames and the drama. Right now there is no phoenix and no rising. You will struggle to sleep, eat, and sometimes breathe. Your body will betray you. Your mind also. Only your soul can hold on—maybe—but it's a nebulous thread that is hard to feel tethered to. No amount of meditation will get you through this.

The injuries and trauma of your past are nothing compared to the wild assault you are experiencing now. Your person left you. This leaving has undone everything you thought you knew about how to be a human in the world. You are being punched in the teeth. Nothing has prepared you to withstand such assault. You don't get to keep your teeth, much less your dignity.

Your body will let you know how not okay you are. You will develop generalized anxiety. The life you've lived up till now, that was relatively free of worry, is over. You didn't know what it was to perseverate or revisit the past. Until now, you were good in a crisis. Once upon a time you thought of yourself as "chill" and present. Other people turned to you. You were reliable. You never fully got how a person could let themselves be completely gripped by crushing anxiety, but you were a good listener. You hung in there, witnessing other people's paralyzing worry without really understanding. Sweetheart, you had no way of knowing what it's like. Now you do.

There is no soothing this quaking body. You know now that your heart will never be the same. The timbre and rhythm, the spaciousness you used to feel in there, are all forever changed. The way a landslide changes the shape of a river, boulders now choke the arteries leading to your heart chambers. The blood flow is squeezed through a narrower passage, the constriction constant and painful.

You will cry for hours curled in the bottom of the shower. The apartment you've rented is tiny, the shower a little cubby that barely fits your body. The shower curtain sticks to your back as you turn to soap up. Curled in the bottom, your limbs spill over the edges. Water pours out onto the tiles for hours. You will mop up the puddles later. Your landlords worked hard on the flooring. For now, you scream till you lose your voice.

You'll quietly apologize on your Zoom calls the next day. The sorry comes out in a pitiful hoarse whisper. "I must be getting sick," you'll say.

You never quite break a bone in your hand punching things. You don't ever damage drywall. You have a very clear understanding of how people might feel compelled to slash tires. You spend a bit of time contemplating exactly how it would be done. You wonder if a Swiss army knife would do the trick, or if you would need a serrated blade. How exactly would you make the first puncture? This line of thinking offers a welcome distraction from how bottomless you feel. At least there is a start, middle, and end to this inquiry.

You will cope. Goodness knows you will cope. You will devise plans. You will offer yourself a survival regimen. You will pray. You will bow. You will consult your ancestors and spirit guides. You will dance and do drugs. You will write endlessly. The outrage spills onto page after page. You will light candles. You will hold the stones and the crystals. Anything, anything to help you heal. You will have hits of insight. You will meditate. Lord, the good baby Jesus will be proud of you for how deeply you will meditate. So tightly you will cling to these threads, though they are only threads. Nothing actually binds you to anything.

Your friends will be there for you. They will rock with you on the phone. They will help you feel your feet and orient you to the colors and shapes in the room. They will help you tap your chest. They will croon, "Sweetie, sweetie, I'm right here with you." But they are a plane ride away. You will know you are loved. More than loved, you are held.

You are blessed with the ability to make deep soul friends. It's a legacy from your dead mother. Your mother had friends who held her hair while she puked on her deathbed. You too have friends holding your hair and wiping your forehead. They show up, over and over, listening to your stories. You ruminate and grind.

"What she did, what she did, what she did."

"See my hurt. See my hurt. See my hurt."

The longing to feel witnessed, seen, and perhaps absolved is insatiable. But the one person whose witnessing matters most you will not get. You know this intellectually, but your body does not. So you ruminate and churn. You contemplate giving your friends a punch card like you get at the coffee shop. A hole punch every time they listen to you repeat the story of your misery. After ten punches they get a free toaster oven.

You've been studying Buddhism and meditating for too long not to recognize this for what it is: the desperate longing for things to be different from what they are. Your resistance is admirable.

The sticky hands of your kids are the only touch you feel against your skin. They sleep in bed with you. You spend nights sandwiched between their sweaty bodies, your brain a whir of lawyering. You compose anthems, poems, letters. You strategize. You spent fifteen years anchored to this person; you can't stop now. The lawyering—the prosecuting—occupies your brain from two to five a.m. every night, churning out a laundry list of items you want her to know, things you want her to feel, arguments you still need to make, wrongs that need to be held aloft for the light to penetrate. Your innocence is impenetrable. She must know what she's done.

You lie ravaged and awake, your brain gnawing away. It could be the hormones. You are, of course, thrust into menopause. The stress of chemotherapy caused your mom's menopause early. Perhaps you are being handed menopause as a way to understand that this stress is untenable for your body. Your body shuts down its estrogen production and drops you off the cliff, your hormones hurtling into the abyss along with everything else.

You will cry on the floor of a bookstore in Capitol Hill in Seattle. One of your beloveds will hold your hand as you read a kids' divorce book. Your own kids have been hanging on, believing their parents will get back together. You have, too. You will never find the words on your own to tell them it is permanent because you cannot believe it is true. You buy the book and walk out into the busy street. The book under your arm is to make up for the frozen silence they got from you as a couple. After rehearsed words one Saturday morning telling them you wouldn't be living together, your ex walked out the door. They have barely seen you in the same room since. There was no planning or contemplation to this divorce. Its sudden rupture matched in intensity by the freeze that followed, as shattering and complete as the childhood trauma you and your ex have stored in your bodies. You had hopes for this trauma to unwind before it was too late. It's now too late.

There will never be a neat story of how this pairing unraveled. There is only the desperate complication of two humans trying to stay open, to drop the entanglements and defenses so tightly tethered to who they think they need to be. Two hurting humans, deep in survival, thrashing for air.

Your kids are waiting patiently for you. Occasionally they ask how long you are going to be separated, but this line of questioning comes less and less frequently. The Saturday morning you told them Mom and Mae were emptying each other's buckets was long ago. In their world, you take a time-out to calm down. You say you are sorry, usually in a fake voice. You get back on the trampoline and bounce again. These two brothers, so close in age they get called twins all the time, recover this way with each other twenty times a day. They don't know about what's impossible to recover from. How do you tell a six-year-old there is no coming back?

You sob some more.

In the midst of all this you will find a lover. Perhaps even a few. There is the sparky hilarious one in a faraway city. You are both caregivers for a parent with dementia; the rage, heartbreak, and roller coaster of that unique experience brings you into intimacy that isn't warranted. You share too much too fast. Your heart skips when they show up in your messages. Anything to make you smile or feel loved. Their texts are spot-on. You almost do a desperate flight change to go meet this person, but don't want to bust this bubble. You compose mini-novellas over text. The flurry of exchange is intoxicating.

Then there is the Seattle one. Tattooed chest, new top surgery that is hot and intriguing. They are available for a walk. You walk, and then fuck against a wall on a public beach. No one is obviously watching, but exhibitionism is a turn-on. As is their body. The chemistry is undeniable. Your body is screaming for sex.

With your partner, you slowly rotted. You made sense of it as the slow drying up into middle age, into tension that couldn't be breached through touch. The hurt was too deep. It's been over three years since anyone other than yourself gave you an orgasm.

You get on a plane for your second date. You are explicit about your red flags. They are big. They are waving furiously in the wind. You are an emotional mess. They know this. They are up for it.

In the week before your date, you leave a letter for your ex, begging, pleading for the possibility of repair. The two of you have basically stopped communicating. You see her traces around the house. The beer cans and pizza boxes in the recycling. The two of you are switching in and out of the house, week on, week off with the kids. The kids are becoming more scarce about how they talk about her. They can see that every word pierces you. She's been an immobile rock. The last time you talked, you asked her not to contact you again until she could hold a thread of kindness for you in her heart. You know this means you may not hear from her for months. You follow her ghost around the house; you feel the weight of her in the bed she vacated the night before. The house swap is not healthy, but you can't contemplate it any other way. You've adjusted to so much. You aren't sure you can adjust to her actually leaving the house.

You leave the letter on the counter.

Then you get on the plane.

The new lover fucks you in the airport parking lot. You drive out to the mountains and find a hot spring to camp beside. On the drive you entwine your fingers. Touch feels good and strange. You talk about things, your kids, your exes. You dance your chess pieces out onto the board. There is resonance. You laugh. Maybe this will be more than just fucking. Maybe not.

You find yourself hungry and empty. Your body is aching to be filled. You are so unsatiated that you can fuck for hours. Your new lover is floored. They haven't met anyone who could outlast them before. It occurs to you that you might outlast everyone you ever sleep with from here forward. How else will you drown out the echoes of the emptiness that has taken up residence in your body? Under the endorphins there is a layer of grim determination. Every minute that your body is filled with the new lover's dick is a moment you are not ruminating. Being removed from the pit of your mind is a gift you can't ever calibrate. It's necessary. And so you fuck. And fuck some more.

But no silicone dick can fill the yawning future in front of you. You take in the new lover's fist. You haven't had your cunt filled with a whole hand in probably twenty years. Your ex's hands were huge, much too big. You can't specifically remember who the last person was to put their whole hand inside you like this. You suck in deep. You can feel their knuckles fill you to your throat. Your edges close around their wrist bones and you scream.

It's a different scream from the one on the floor of the shower. This one is defiant. In the midst of the wreckage you will fucking survive. You have a lover's fist inside of you to prove how much you can take. You will not be broken. The rocking, the holding, the shuddering is all necessary for your survival.

At the moment, it seems like the only way to metabolize this pain.

You are explicit. You don't promise anything, even after you come. It's a bad habit you have: endorphins flooding your body and promising the world. You've done it before. Even inviting some cishet boy who you only sort of liked to follow you to Brazil while you were still sitting on his cock. The afterglow of orgasms is a powerful tonic for you. This time you are restrained, proving that you have learned something as you age. So here you are. Promising only to be present. Promising only that you would like to fuck again. Promising to be nothing, and maybe everything to this person. You aren't imagining how they will rescue you from your predicament. There is no way out.

Far-flung lovers are what you want.

But when you return home, opened, empty, and sore, maybe you want more.

Only you live someplace where it's impossible for you to disappear into anonymous fucking. Your closest potential dates on the apps are 208 miles away.

The texts from the faraway hottie with the dementia parent are not enough to keep your endorphins up. You are afraid of leading the Seattle lover on. And so you bide. And mope. After a while you stop imagining the next orgasms.

The truth is, the new lover made you miss your wife. How she knew exactly where to put her thumbs and her tongue to make you come. You've forgotten all your own quirks, it's been so long. Passing the instruction manual on to a new lover while trying to be hot feels daunting.

You miss the ex's plug-and-play approach to sex. The matter-of-factness of the goal. There was something pedestrian about your love life. Despite your disappointment at the lack of adventure, the lights-out, after-shower, horizontal-on-a-bed sex was comforting. She screwed up her face any time you mentioned your raunchy, kinky fantasies. Eventually you stopped. You had other, deeper places you needed to grow together. You let hope take over, thought maybe your sex life would come along once you had mended some of the rifts. It was enough that she knew where to put her thumbs. Your ex would never tie you to a tree and fuck your ass from behind, under the full strawberry moon of the summer solstice.

You came back from your sexpedition raw and pink. Evidence of your pale body stretched under the sun while your new lover fucked you in the shallow water of the hot spring. Fucking you ruthlessly and endlessly in a way that you wanted. In your eagerness to feel, the excruciating burn of ripe red skin added sensation to the experience. Days later, you rubbed flakes of skin off in little rolls in the shower, your body shedding itself. Your kids noticed your sunburnt belly and chest. "Skinny dipping," you said. "I forgot to put on sunscreen."

The first time you and your ex fucked, you got sunburnt as well. You went off into the desert and camped beside the truck, forgetting about the backpacking trip you were going to take. Days of bodies splayed out under the sun. The complete abandon of caution searing your futures together. After days of sandy camping and fucking with no thought of sunscreen, you blearily wandered the grocery store aisles, looking for aloe vera. In the motel room you squirted green gel on her back while she lay on the bleached white sheets, then fucked some more, grimacing through your screaming skin to scream into each other's necks before you got on a plane the next morning.

Before that desert adventure, your ex had milky skin. Forever after, her back was speckled with big, blotchy freckles. She left behind the purity of her skin under your spell. Marked forever. The freckles will be a testament to whoever next digs their fingers into the broad expanse of her back. You wonder if she would shed her back freckles to erase the memories of you. Does she truly want the fresh start she appears to be creating so frantically?

Eventually, over Zoom with the lawyer present, your ex tells you it's over. Permanently. This is months after your letter on the counter. Months of radio silence from her. Months of peddling hope, peddling disbelief, peddling a notion that adults needed to make this decision, not traumatized inner children flooded by fear. You are outraged. Your anger is righteous. You cover the territory of fight response; she expertly covers flight and freeze. You are obsessed with the notion that your children deserve more. You are obsessed with the notion that you are searing the legacy of family trauma into your kids' psyches. The trauma of ugly divorce and alcoholism that came in the generation before, trickling down and ensuring your children will never find secure attachment. You are flooded with shame that you did not, or could not, slow her down.

You cry in the grocery store, when your friend finally drags you there, at nine p.m. At this hour, you are unlikely to see anyone you know. You won't have to watch acquaintances duck into different aisles to avoid having to see your broken face.

Your friend gently suggests a few things you might eat. Frozen meals, easy to prepare. Stuff that won't go bad in the fridge and with some nutritional value. It's impossible to imagine you will be able to care for yourself. You know a box of cookies every other day does not cut it.

Your ex is beloved in the community. You cannot help but wonder what she is telling people. No one ever expected that you would separate. You have long been the token queers among straight outdoorsy people who love to demonstrate their openness. She, compartmentalizing and appearing fine, didn't miss a step. She's been at all the barbecues and soccer games, joking and jovial with other parents. You make up a story that you are the broken one. And so people duck into different grocery store aisles, and turn quickly at the schoolyard pickup, to avoid having to see your broken face.

You weep and weep and weep and weep for the losses.

The person who helped you labor as you birthed your first child, the person who dug her nails into your arm till you bruised as she pushed your second child into your waiting hands, no longer loves you. At almost fifty, you know you will not be loved through the formative chunk of your life again. That was the bulk event. The main course. There may be mature and jaded love, there may be wise love, but you will never again experience the kind of unadulterated, hopeful love that could carry hot-air balloons across the ocean.

Your friend who is also going through a divorce texts you frequent *My therapist says . . .* missives. In one, the therapist has said, "When you heal your attachment wounds, you might not actually need to find partnership again." This idea fills your body with relief, both because you live in a small rural town where you are unlikely to partner again, and because you love even the faintest notion that healing attachment wounds might be possible.

You wonder what you might say if you could talk to your younger, ebullient self. The one who wore a red wedding dress with one strap and floated, high on the certainty of the path they were on. "Be careful," maybe. "This person will not always bring out the best in you."

Because your ex will make you an ugly version of you. You will do things that make you hate yourself. And no, you will not love her more today than yesterday, every day. That was a cute part of your vows, but that phase will end.

At some point, in therapy, you will realize that your wife actually left you the week after your mother died, even though she hung on for another year before pulling the plug. This realization will give you immense compassion for yourself and for all the ways you've raged and lashed out. Of course you raged. You never got to grieve your mom; you were so busy trying to hang on to your relationship. The double whammy—your mom dying and your partner emotionally leaving you immediately afterward—was too much for your system to handle.

After your mom died, a bustling inner manager took over, fixated on the agenda of saving your marriage. "If I heal us I will be okay." The manager knew that losing your mom and your wife in the same week would destroy you. Instead, in those months after your mother's death, you drove to Baja with your soon-to-be ex-wife for her long-needed sabbatical, the kids in the back of the car. Your manager kept busy finding school for your kids, second-hand bikes to ride around on. Christmas presents so they would feel some celebration inside their crumbling family. All of this busy-ness kept you from having to see that your wife was already gone. Kept you from having to do the monumental task of grieving two losses at once. So you grieved neither and clung hard to some version of reality you believed was possible.

The clinging and managing held you hostage. You forgot what it was to feel wild and holy and alive.

When you finally realized there was no possibility of repair and your wife was leaving for good, you unhinged. Of course you did. You had no family left. You were estranged from your sister. Your dad was in long-term care, and although he was a sweet and tender presence in your life, holding his hand and listening to his incoherent babbling was not the same as being enveloped by a robust and unconditional parental love.

In some ways it was a blessing. Your parents loved your ex-wife unconditionally, in a way that made her uncomfortable. She never understood how freely and unquestionably she was their daughter. If your mother had been alive, your father cognizant, when she left you, they would have grieved the loss like they would a child killed in a car accident.

So you did that grieving for them. Your wife had left you emotionally the minute she walked out the door that fateful Saturday morning. It was a leaving so sudden and complete, your body responded like she had been hit by a Mack truck. Your cells locked around the imprint of a horrific accident.

Her presence in your therapy sessions on Zoom felt like seeing a ghost. She was so shut down and gone, there was no shred of her left. She made it easy to forget the person you had fallen in love with. That human had vaporized.

When your new lover, the one from Seattle, asked about your scars, you told the story of your rag-doll free fall down a slope in the Waddington range. Your ice axe flinging in your hand. How you didn't self-arrest. Now you think: Perhaps there is no way you could have. Perhaps you are oriented to surrender. Perhaps you allow things to happen and don't believe you can actually influence the outcome. And so you had tumbled, head over ankles over backpack, winding up in a bloody heap at the bottom of the slope, your face mangled by your ice axe. You described to your lover how you put your fingers to the shredded skin of your mouth, how the blood seeped, how you thought, "Well, I've spent the first half of my life as a relatively good-looking person; I can spend the second half with a distorted face." In the end the scar on your lip was only mildly distracting, and all that was exposed was your vanity.

Your new lover listened to the story, tracing the shape of your lips with their thumb, and then licked your mouth. You wanted to swallow their thick tongue, to swallow them whole. Rag-doll down the slope out of control. Perhaps that is your state of equilibrium? Everything tumbling and crashing, no ice axe in the snow to isolate, to make any sense or order of the chaos.

Eventually you stop praying. The altar, the astrology journal, your ancestors looking at you, none of this anchors you anymore. The free fall feels imminent. You wonder how long and how far you will rag-doll.

You spend a week in the mountains walking by yourself. With each footfall you chant "accept, accept, accept." As your heel strikes the rocks, the finality reverberates up your leg bones and into your gut. You feel like vomiting the whole week, your body letting you know what acceptance will taste like in the back of your throat.

After the call with the lawyer where she told you it was final, you know what to do. You tell her, "We can do this." You ask for time. In person. She comes over the next day. It's the first time she has set foot in your apartment. She comes in soft, grateful that you are letting her in. You realize it's the first time you have felt her truly open and present since one particular day on a beach in Baja, more than a year and a half ago. Her face is familiar, and beloved. Not the stone mask it's been for the last agonizing year.

You collapse in tears and she holds you. Finally. You are getting what you've desperately needed: somewhere to lay your weary and grieving head. You've needed this since your mother died, since she left you. How strange that the person who has terrorized you this way is the person giving you the one thing you most need. A final parting gift.

You know this moment matters. You are held by something in, through, and beyond you. You are walking each other down the aisle, only in the opposite direction. You offer each other blessings. You offer commitments. Yours to her is to let her go. Fifteen years ago you promised to care for her. Today, your promise is the opposite. You will let her be. You promise to no longer need anything from her, to prod her, to hope for her healing or presence or anything else that your system had been hungrily railing after for years. Your gift to her is to let her be exactly who she is. In her full freedom and sovereignty.

You hold her one last time. Letting her go is excruciating. She walks out the door.

Of course, there is a stark contrast between the closure and crying in the apartment and her actually moving out of the house. Her stone-faced immobility is back. You had hoped for a week of laughing and crying, surrounded by stacks of boxes in the basement. "You take this. No, let's burn that."

Instead she walks in, for the two hours she has begrudgingly agreed to, just as you're reading a letter she wrote on your eighth wedding anniversary. Her untidy handwriting tells you how proud she was of the learning and growing you were doing together. How grateful she was to you for pushing the two of you into hard, growing work. That she was here for it. How excited and proud she was to think of the two of you evolving in the years to come.

You pull the framed wedding vows off the bedroom wall. Not long after your wedding, she'd found a local artist to write out the vows in fancy calligraphy and put them in nice frames. Not until she walked through the door for those begrudging two hours did you realize how unhinged you were. You stop yourself from throwing the heavy frame at her. Broken glass wouldn't have elicited any reaction from her anyway. Instead your body shakes as if the imagined broken glass is raining down over your head. The betrayal is so complete. Not the least because she couldn't say the one thing you wanted to hear: "I'm sorry I broke my promise. I'm sorry I am not going to raise these kids with you."

The kids learn their parents will never get back together. They try on the word *divorce*. At the family meeting, they don't want to listen to your carefully planned words. They know what is coming, and so they bounce and crash into each other on the trampoline, laughing in high-pitched voices that aren't their own. Of course they go off the rails. It's the only sane way to respond to an impossible circumstance.

You tell your kids you are devastated that you are doing this to them. Later, your wife chastises you, telling you that word is too big for them, that you're burdening them with your shit. Who knows what the right thing to say to kids is. You are increasingly numb. You realize they will be parented by two wholly different entities that reside on two different planets. The intellectualizing part of you can say it's good for kids to know paradox, that many things can be true at the same time. It's also good that you are teaching them young that they can survive in circumstances they don't like. Climate catastrophe will demand this capacity from them in the decades to come. You are preparing them.

What you want instead is to wrap them in the security of a two-parent household. For them to know they have the same thing other kids have, even if they are the only kids in town with two moms. There is no longer a container for them. This betrayal feels like death.

You will experience the ache of not recognizing your children's smells. They smell of different detergent and shampoo. You've already experienced the shock of her giving them haircuts without warning you. You go to pick them up at school and experience the gut punch of not seeing your kid. The long, tangled curls are gone, and your child's shorn head looks like every other small head running after the soccer ball. The grief of losing your kids for half their lives is more than you can bear. Acknowledging this stops your breath.

You will learn to drop below your head. Your head wrestles with the question: "Will I be okay?" The answer sends your heart rate through the roof. But when you learn to drop that question down into the bottom of your belly, into the bowl of your pelvis, different things happen. The question changes into something with fewer words. There is a felt sense of rushing blood and warmth extending in, through, and out of your body. It's as if the universe is gently holding your feet to the fire. Sweet One, don't concern yourself with such trivial matters, the universe says.

You are held.

You are held.

You are held.

You will scrub the walls, repaint the house. Crisp white. Fresh. Very mature. You will find there is nothing that erases the ghosts. You see her and feel her standing by the sink. Even though she has not looked you in the eye with softness for over a year, your cells still remember her.

You beg her back into therapy with the hope of not embedding the trauma of this divorce into your kids. Your first couples therapist had been a disaster, as surprised as you were by the sudden departure of your wife, and clearly out of her depth. You find a new one that helps you both stay in the room. Teaspoon by teaspoon, you are learning to feel a sliver of safety in your ex's presence on the Zoom screen. It is therapy that came a year too late.

Your task is sloughing off the anchor of her, the impossible work of unravelling your codependence. You must call yourself back to yourself. You are the only one who can hold you. No one else will save you from this. No one else is there anymore to take you to the hospital at two a.m. It is only you—to make the lunches, to hold your kids' despair and withdrawal. You don't have a compatriot to help them make sense of how the bottom is falling out of their lives.

At almost fifty years old you are learning, in a grueling way, how to take care of yourself. The task is monumental, especially when you have unraveled this far. And it is true, you may not survive this. But you will go on. This sadness will engulf you. Slowly, slowly, you start to allow it to fully swallow you, feeding yourself fully to the gargantuan ache. In a way, this surrender is healing.

This is not a missive about how to survive. There are no silver linings. If you make it out, it will be ugly. But you will go on. Stupidly, desperately, you will go on. You will learn how to hold yourself, even if only for a sliver of a second. Your friend's therapist says this: "People never think they will get through, but they always do." You feel the weight of this message on your phone cradled in your hand, standing in the grocery store parking lot. The text is not yet reassuring.

One day.

One day, Sweet One, you will find out if what the therapist says is true.

For today, you will go on.

Words Are Spells

NAILAH ROSE

Maybe it started with the sun. His routine complaint that the room was too bright in the morning and you needed blackout curtains. Your response:

I want to wake up with the light. It's like a natural alarm clock for me.

Silence. Get up to get ready for the day. And repeat.

Weeks later, he began falling asleep on the basement couch. One night became two. Two nights became seven. A budding argument shape-shifted into muted acceptance. Again. You chalk it up to the tales of queer polyamorous thriving, the ones you sought out to make sense of the world. Fuck the system and status quo living. You were both getting your needs met, and there are couples you know who sleep in separate rooms. So, it's all good, right?

The lies we tell to save ourselves from speaking.

You, a save-the-world witch, hell-bent on self-sacrifice. Him, a love theorist using study as a shield. Individually, you each survived a lot of sorrowful, sweet, complex family drama that threatened to bury you alive. Together, you made a promise to always center choice and never obligation. It felt liberatory. Yet over time, the words twisted into cavernous hollows, always with a floor in between. You convinced yourself the conversationless chasm you had dug yourselves into was okay, and your actions still communicated your love and care for one another. The questions like "Where's your husband?" at work events and family gatherings was because the straights didn't understand power couple behavior or the unique truth of our love. He was probably getting the same questions.

But silence is a spell too, is it not?

OBLIGATION:

an act or course of action to which a person is morally or legally bound

a duty or commitment

Your foundation was strong, sealed by ceremonial magic you fought for, designed, acquiesced to, and were transformed by. On that rainy day in May, you wore heels and a skirt publicly for the first time. You both called on your ancestors, were prayed over, and danced until daylight. You reminded your people that Nailah is the only name you'll accept. Your families showered you with love. The world suddenly became a place centering Black queer power—power you had sought to feel and embody for most of your life. This was world-building through the art of ritual, spoken aloud with conviction and sealed in a contractual agreement with the state.

But how did we get there? Maybe it started with those words. The first ones. Not the ones about karaoke or your favorite video games. No—the ones that came after your yearning eyes watched intently for over a year, trying to understand how he moved, how he shaped his life. You grasped for meaning in his sea of syllables, searching for what might stick. What might touch the quiet floor of your heart and make a forever home there. He said them first:

"I want to build wealth with you."

Not the ones you expected. But how dreamy, right? A desire to grow and blossom so abundantly that you nourish generations. But each of us carries our own definitions of the words we use, or perhaps we choose a definition that aligns with our own understanding of the world. Over time, the fine print became more clear, and you realized your definitions were different. His was a dream of acquisition. Yours was a dream of relationship. Viewed together, they were disconnected stories in conflict, desperately seeking resolution. Thus, you waited. Remember, your foundation was strong. So, you'd get there, right?

The lies we tell to save ourselves from asking.

CHOICE:

an act of selecting or making a decision when faced with two or more possibilities

Maybe it continued with your bodies. They just . . . forgot each other. They stopped being curious, stopped seeking connection. Each of you primarily respected the other's space while evolving in your own individual journeys. His body, caught in work compulsion and unknown to you fully. Your body, trapped in a void of impostor syndrome and the depths of ongoing grief. You can't save everyone. You can barely save yourself.

And something more. A whisper from childhood, echoing softly in your mind. Emerging again after a long stint with the oncology department.

How can I even trust my body anymore? It betrayed me.

Again after that weekend in the mountains with Maria where you held hands and drank special tea, and the world became a kaleidoscope of stars within infinite darkness.

The depths are where the answers lie. Jump in, my love.

Something old and achingly beautiful begging for release. Begging for you to get to know her. To trust her. To let her lead. The wedding was just the beginning. Earrings and scarves became lipstick and dresses, suddenly becoming life jackets to her. Portals for her to peek through.

You can trust this.

Allowing folks to "he" you was just another accommodation, another expression of self-doubt. You were learning that your magic was only as powerful as the boundaries you held, the belief you invoked, and the aligned action you took. The whispers became louder.

You can trust yourself.

You were learning stronger boundaries, so you allowed it no more. You initiated conversations with your sexual partners about the ways you could no longer "butch up" for your rendezvous. Your flavor of gender expansiveness was becoming less liminal. You belonged to a universe of femme genders—the same universe that you spoke your belonging to in second grade, that your imagination celebrated and honored.

Through all of this, you did feel his love and care through his actions. A glimmer of appreciation as you walked down the street in a full-length gown. A nudge to put that dress back on before your anniversary dinner. Still, there was an absence of words. A lack of inquiry and presence you chalked up to his busyness. Legal name and gender-marker changes were profoundly solo journeys—no questions, no celebrations, just acceptance.

You began making requests. Accommodating less. Your needs were getting clearer: You needed more time, more intimacy, more connection. Things he didn't have the capacity for but said he would work on.

You loved him. You would wait.

The lies we tell ourselves to save ourselves from knowing.

Maybe it swelled with Spirit. You do believe you called him to you. A baby witch who was practicing setting intention, you wrote down words in red ink and placed them in your prayer box.

I wish for love and partnership, fulfilling me in my highest good.

For a long while, it did just that, offering an anchor of stability while aerating the soil enough to let more of the light in. It brought you to one of the highest proclamations of your own power, and it gave you space to run away to the woods when it all fell apart. It encouraged you to deepen spiritual intimacy with your beloveds, who helped you remember the purpose you were so prone to forgetting.

The more you leaned on Spirit, the more truth came. Your reflections became more honest, your words clearer. Your magic grew alongside your transition, as lessons in impermanence and interdependence appeared repeatedly. Your closest relationships rooted you deep into the core of the earth, offering a bounty of sweetness and platonic love promising to witness and protect you. New relationships emerged, one an unexpected dance of ecstasy and reverence that healed long-dead parts of you. Other relationships ended, and while in tears at your altar one afternoon, a familiar tugging pulled at your mind. You grabbed your journal as words flooded in.

There are lineages of women who have loved men despite their shortcomings, their journeys. Who gave more of themselves, who stretched them.

Who knew the imbalance and still loved anyway.

Know that this is the labor you choose.

You are not breaking cycles here.

If you choose it, let the labor strengthen you,

in radical honesty, in boundaries, in conflict, in clarity.
And always make space to tend to yourself.
Your heart is a tender and open one.

Sometimes the containers we thought could hold us no longer have the capacity to. And there were signs. He broke his wedding ring twice in a year. His trips became longer, expensive gifts appearing in his absence. The trips you took together were more acrimonious. You'd be together in place, but you couldn't sense him anymore, as if his spirit was anywhere but here, with you. But he was working on it. He said he was working on it. You told yourself he was working on it. You believed he was working on it.

Soon thereafter, you said yes to a life-changing invitation. You quit your job and went on a month-long ancestral remembering journey with your spiritual beloved, Ngina. The land showed you many things, including visions of you that couldn't be unseen. Upon your return, you shared that the word "husband" didn't quite work for you anymore, that you were considering taking new steps to affirm your gender, and that you wanted him to meet a new partner of yours. He celebrated you with his words in ways you'd never heard before. It made your heart sing.

The next month, you returned to the recipe for a three-day spiritual bath, given to you a year and a half ago by a trusted Hoodoo practitioner. As you mixed the herbs and took the bath each night, you set the intention to release what no longer served you. On the third evening, after your bath and during a planned date night, he said he had no more capacity or will to be in your marriage. When you asked for clarity, he noted that your transition was part of it. And in that moment—realizing this was not an invitation to a conversation but a cold, direct decision—you broke. An unfamiliar rage made a home in you. It still lives here.

DIVORCE:
the legal dissolution of a marriage by a court or other competent body

Perhaps this was always just a business transaction. A legal commitment to mutual upward mobility and a shared life while somehow still living completely separate ones. He had achieved the wealth he desired, so your contract was no longer necessary. But what about the contract of your spirits? The prayers over your lives, the ritual? Perhaps your leaps of faith terrified him. Perhaps you shared too many needs, too many revelations. Years of muted acceptance crashing open and flooding the space between you. Perhaps ultimately your spirit, too, needed a new place to call home.

It was always precarious though, wasn't it? The sporadic feathery touches, the all-consuming work talk, the silence you both committed to, the distance between dream and reality. Centering choice but never obligation became a prison you'd bound yourselves to. Maybe you should have seen it coming. You didn't.

The disentangling has been a painful one. Legal documents arrive with deadnames on them. Preparing for scheduling hearings and mediations catapults you toward old states of disembodiment. Do you "butch up" for the state? Will it keep you safe from violence? Is that even possible anymore?

You already know the answers here, my love.

Years of unaddressed conflict emerge in new and surprising ways. In those moments, you're endlessly proud of how clear and formidable you've become. You've held several funerals for the versions of you that trusted his words. That accommodated consistently and labored without acknowledgement. That felt but didn't ask. Knew but didn't speak.

When grief is bigger than your body, it splits. A jagged tear from crown to creation, loosening the carefully organized tower you built up inside you. But in that tear, you also make a way for more truth and aliveness than you ever thought possible.

Turns out, all along, the light you sought to wake up to was your own.

Late Bloomer

R. M. H.

It took me two tries to leave my husband.

The first time was planned, with a sit-down and a "we need to talk."

I told him I was a lesbian. It wasn't true, but it was the closest I could come to addressing the issue of my identity. My therapist seemed sure that was what was going on, and I wanted something that would feel nonnegotiable: a nice, clear *It's not you, it's me.*

"I think we should separate," I said. "I've realized some things about myself since getting sober, and I'm not happy."

"I'll kill myself," he said.

He said he would do anything to keep me, to support me in exploring my identity; he said I didn't have to leave, we could open up the marriage, I could find a way to be myself within the marriage.

I said I would stay, and I tried to believe that he meant it when he said he wanted me to feel comfortable being open with him. I messaged my therapist and told her I had decided to stay in my marriage and therefore no longer needed her services. She never replied. I cut my hair and experimented with binding for the first time since college. Whenever my husband hugged me, he would feel the back of my shirt to see whether I was wearing a binder or a bra. When we were intimate, he would touch my hairy legs or my short hair and recoil.

What I want to say is that he became paranoid and controlling after that conversation; but what is more true is that this was nothing new. I had already spent the prior ten years keeping myself as small as possible, doing my best to fit what he seemed to want from me. He didn't like opera; I stopped listening to opera. He preferred long hair; I kept mine long. I stopped humming around the house, cooked only the things he wanted, let him choose the movies and the restaurants. I dressed to please him. I avoided Pride events and churches because he didn't approve of either one. I didn't read library books in bed. I went to bed when he wanted me to, even when I worked at a bakery and left for work before dawn. Before we even moved in together, I had already given up art in favor of a stable career to support his goals, so what did it matter if I also chose my clothes with an eye to the things he liked?

As long as I did all of these things, we fit just fine.

That wasn't true, of course. He was very unhappy and prone to angry explosions. They were rarely directed at me, but I learned how to spot the warning signs and became hypervigilant about his moods, trying so hard to anticipate what I was supposed to be doing that I lost the ability to make any decisions on my own. I learned never to ask questions and never to challenge him. I hid my thoughts and avoided making friends, because I couldn't deal with the prospect of introducing them to him.

I avoided even talking about him to coworkers. My boss once told me that if she hadn't been at my wedding, she wouldn't have believed I was married. I told my husband this because I thought it was funny, and maybe he would appreciate knowing I wasn't gossiping about him.

"Why the fuck would she say that?" he answered.

I'm being terribly unfair here. My husband wasn't a monster, and it wasn't always bad. I was hiding things, I was angry, I was an alcoholic. When I talk about my marriage, I make it sound like I was completely passive, as if I did nothing but meekly flinch away from my awful husband. That isn't true. We had friends, we went places. Every few years or so, I would decide the argument was worth it and cut my hair. I ran in marathons, I sang in choirs. He didn't exactly approve of either one—he despised both running and group activities of all varieties—but he was also strangely proud of me, at least in public. I say that, but then I remember how clear it was that he viewed my hobbies as an imposition.

I want so badly for it to be only his fault or only my fault. It would have been so much easier if he had always been only awful.

It feels unfair to blame him for being blindsided by that first conversation. Of course he thought I was happy. I had done everything in my power to keep him from noticing anything different. How could he understand that my flawed attempt at coming out was more about my identity than about any desire for a different partner? It only makes sense that his first question after my announcement was whether I was seeing someone else, and that his second question was whether I wanted to be seeing someone else.

The answer to both was "no."

I stayed another two years, and I tried very hard to understand his feelings. I had hurt him, I told myself. Of course it was going to take time for him to trust me again. His insistence on doing everything together was about his desire for closeness, not control. Of course, he only wanted to come to the concerts to support my singing (he left at intermission, satisfied that I hadn't been lying about where I spent my Monday nights). Of course he objected when I wanted to attend a queer singing event in my hometown ("I'm just afraid those people will queer you up"). Of course he needed me to dress more femininely to reassure him (he found a boutique named Feel Like a Woman! and gave me a gift certificate). Of course he needed to stalk my social media (what did I have to hide, after all?), of course, of course, of course.

Wouldn't it be nice if this was the part where I finally stood my ground and accepted his invitation to be more open—the part where we both opened our hearts to each other and offered all our love and vulnerability and decided to make it work? I could tell him I was trans, something dude-adjacent, if not quite a man, and he could tell me how happy he was for me and that he'd realized some things about himself, and we would embrace and live happily ever after.

That's not what happened.

I stayed at work as much as I could, and I deleted all of the social media accounts he had found. I started new ones with less guessable names. I wrote to virtual advice columns and read horoscopes and begged the universe for some sort of sign that would make it okay for me to finally leave. I wasted a truly ridiculous amount of time hoping for fairytale solutions: miraculous time travel, Narnia doors, alien abductions. I hoped I would get into a car accident or be diagnosed with a terminal illness, and that would finally somehow be the excuse I needed to tell him to leave so I could spend some portion of my life free of him.

Instead, I told him we should try for a baby. I gave my men's clothes to charity and grew my hair back out. I kept having unprotected sex with him, telling him that I was still "his woman," and biting my tongue as he made increasingly hostile statements about the queer community. One day I walked into the living room and he was lying on the couch watching a YouTube video of some right-wing ghoul talking about trans people. The person on the video said, "These freaks would have you deny the basic biological truth that men cannot become women and that women cannot become men!"

My husband looked at me with rage on his face and said, "He's fucking right about that, at least."

Somehow, I've gotten this far without talking about addiction. I'm an alcoholic, a sober one, but an alcoholic nonetheless. I know there are schools of thought about the use of the term *alcoholic*, thoughts about whether identifying as your addiction is constructive or not, about how strange it is that alcoholism is the only addiction with a special name and whether that leads to unnecessary stigma. I don't care very much. The term fits my experience. I'm more than seven years sober now (apart from the small relapse that I will discuss shortly), but it has not been easy to get here, and it still feels precarious.

The complicated truth of the matter is that I drank to stay in my marriage. I drank to avoid knowing the things about myself that I wasn't ready to know. I drank because I had no hope and because I could not stand what I was feeling. I drank as a slow-motion suicide. All of this is true, but I also think that my relapse may have saved my life.

Now we have arrived at the second time I tried to leave my husband.

I didn't mean to.

Rather, I meant to, but not in the way I did it. The first time I had a plan. I had been about a year sober, and I had an apartment lined up and a bag packed, the essentials stashed in my office at work.

When the second time rolled around, I had become superstitious, half-convinced that the preparation was the reason it didn't work before, sort of like bringing your umbrella to prevent the rain. I needed to talk to him because I had no other choice, but I didn't know what I would do next, just that I couldn't keep going the way I had been.

Remember, of course, that I had told him we could have a baby because that's a method of fixing marriages that's both traditional and foolproof. It was stupid, and I knew it. I'll go ahead and spoil the ending now and say that I didn't get pregnant. He has since accused me of leaving because I thought he would be a bad father, maybe even an abusive one. He's right. I also was in no position to be a good parent.

I avoided sex, and when I couldn't, I would initiate the sort of sex less likely to end in pregnancy. Stress made my periods irregular, and every month I would find myself thinking, *What will I do if I'm pregnant?* I was in our bathroom taking a pregnancy test when the answer came to me.

I'll kill myself.

I'd love to say that this is when I knew we had to talk. I'd love to say that I sat down and was open and honest about everything. I had planned to do that, really. Maybe I hadn't planned to tell him that I was trans, but in my defense, that's because I wasn't completely certain at that point. It doesn't matter what I had planned to say, because it never happened.

Instead, I came home from work and sat in the living room and let him talk to me. I have no memory at all of the conversation, but whatever it was, I could not make myself say anything. That night, I let him fuck me, let him cum inside me, and when that was done, I spent a good hour contemplating my wrists and a razor blade, wondering if I really needed to die, or if I could just make a serious enough attempt to get hospitalized, and whether that would be enough of an excuse to ask for a divorce. I don't think I slept much that night.

The next day, I drank. Just a shot or so from one of his bottles of liquor. After work, I bought a bottle of vodka.

I think I had decided I was going to die, but not right then. My parents and I had grown apart, estranged by my marriage to a man who didn't like them, who didn't seem to share any of their values. They didn't like him either. They didn't think he was good for me. They didn't think I was myself when I was with him. They were absolutely right, and they also had the good sense not to tell me any of this at the time.

However, my father had dementia, and the disease was progressing. My mom needed me, and I wanted to be there for her, but I couldn't find a way to do it. At the very least, though, I could refrain from making it worse by dying right then.

I made a bargain with myself: *I just need to outlive my mother*, I told myself. *Once she's gone, I can go too. I've made it this far. I can make it another twenty years, but I can't do it sober.*

My husband found the bottle. He confronted me about it while I was raking the yard.

"We're trying to have a baby," he said. "I was talking to my brother about fertility treatments just last week! How can we do that if I can't trust you to be sober?"

"I don't want to have a baby," I answered. "I can't be married to you anymore."

We said more. He wanted me to tell him what he'd done wrong. He was shocked, completely blindsided once again, even though we had been there before, literally in the same room. He thought we'd been doing so much better; COVID was making everyone crazy; I was just having some sort of a breakdown. I don't remember most of it.

I walked to the bedroom, threw the contents of a laundry hamper into a bag, and then drove across the country to my parents' house.

A few months before I left, he had picked out a movie: *Cast a Deadly Spell*, which had been billed as a campy '80s horror movie, vaguely Lovecraftian in flavor. This movie features a minor character who is played by a male actor in women's clothing. It's unclear in the narrative whether the character is meant to be a man in drag or a trans woman. It's even less clear whether the writers realize that those aren't the same thing. What is abundantly clear is that they hate this character.

The movie features an extended scene in which the "heroic" protagonist of the film "reveals" the drag/trans character's masculine features and then viciously beats her in a scene that is clearly meant to be comedic.

My husband laughed uproariously through the whole thing.

When the movie was over, he was positively giddy about how much he enjoyed it, and he pressed me over and over for an opinion. I'm still not sure whether he wanted me to agree with him, whether agreement would disprove his suspicions, or whether I was expected to object and give him the excuse to finally have the fight he'd wanted.

"Wasn't that great?" he said.

"It had its moments," I replied.

After I left, he contacted me, of course. Over and over, I would receive text messages begging me to return, outlining increasingly surreal ways that we could make it work, flattery and love-bombing alternating with twelve-page emails detailing everything I had done wrong, then ending with a generous offer to take me back despite how awful I really was. He had noticed the men's clothes and the short hair, he said, and he felt like I was deliberately trying to disgust him, that my presentation was a punishment. He thanked me for how I had stopped doing that.

He sent memes and romantic gifs, message after message, hoping, I assume, for a reaction. They were bizarrely traditional, romantic in a way that had never been a feature of our relationship, so decidedly out of character it was actually surreal.

So, no, I never told him I was trans. I didn't want to watch someone *try* to accept who I was. I had already lived with the barely veiled expression of disgust at a haircut or unshaven legs, or a hat that was somehow too masculine. I had already heard the slurs and the laughter. I had already spent every June vibrating with tension every time a company ran a Pride month ad, just waiting for the inevitable anger.

If I'm truly honest with myself, though, the biggest reason I didn't tell him I was trans was that it didn't feel relevant. It wasn't why I wanted a divorce. I think it is possible for marriage to withstand transition, for people to change in ways that continue to complement each other, to find ways through with love and communication and vulnerability. For me, though, the ways in which I was unable to express my identity and my wishes did not start with my queerness or my gender identity, and they did not stop there.

He figured it out himself, sometime after I left but before the divorce was finalized. I had to make a last visit to the house to pick up a few things before moving back to New Orleans for good. He'd already known, of course, from the social media stalking and everything else, but the voice drop confirmed it.

"I would have tried," he said. "It would have been hard for me, but I would have tried to accept it."

Is it possible that he meant it? Of course it is.

Shame makes it hard to hold onto anger. I'm deeply ashamed of myself for leaving the way I did, for never being brave enough to tell him even a fraction of the truth of who I was, for marrying him in the first place. There were good times, and there were ways in which I grew that I would not have if I hadn't known him. The longer we've been apart, the more I think about the good things, and the harder it is to remember the fear that I felt.

Even harder than that is to convince myself that my fears weren't unfounded simply because none of them came to pass. He never hit me. He rarely even yelled *at* me. There are still holes that he punched in the walls of the house. There are still times that he hurt himself. There were road-rage incidents that almost turned violent. There were racist and homophobic slurs. There were the controlling tendencies that were already escalating. There were guns in the basement. I worried that he would show up at my parents' house, or that he would come to my job with a gun. He told me, in a twelve-page-long email, that my fears were delusional, that I had built him up into a completely different person. I find it very interesting that he apparently had no difficulty conceiving of what my fears might be, when I never told him about any of them.

It's been over two years since the divorce was finalized, more than three since I left. We aren't in contact, and I don't foresee that changing.

For all the times when I tell myself I must have imagined how unhappy I was, there are many more days on which I find myself doing something I would not have believed possible.

I returned to New Orleans, and I see my mom several times a week. She keeps me busy with things that need doing around the house. My transition hasn't been exactly easy for her. She worries about me, about the politics in the state, about her family's reaction. With my dad sick, she probably didn't really need my pile of trauma tossed on top of hers, but her support has never wavered, and I am so lucky to have rebuilt my relationship with her.

Dad passed away a year ago. Sometimes it feels I came back too late, but mostly I count myself incredibly fortunate to have come back when I did. We managed to have some good times in his last couple of years. His dementia was mostly marked by aphasia, and it was always hard to tell how much he understood. A few days after I told my parents I was transitioning, he walked into church and proudly announced that his daughter was going to be a boy now, much the same way he would have said that I had decided to go back to graduate school. He was a great listener to my divorce drama, and his somewhat impaired filter led to memorable feedback like, "Christ, what a miserable bastard," which remains one of the most validating things anyone has ever said to me.

I have friends now, which feels like a strange and wondrous thing after having relied on my husband and his social circle for so many years. During the divorce, I was told that I was making a mistake, that I would be isolated and alone without him, that I wasn't capable of friendship. Recently, I helped a pair of new friends move, and it was one of the proudest achievements of my life.

My husband had always been very concerned about what people might think, and he used that concern as a cudgel against me more than a few times over the years. The relief of living only according to my own values, of being fully myself in all of my strangeness and untidiness, has been immense. Almost daily I find myself doing something I would not have been allowed to do when I was married, from the big, transition-related things—like top surgery, and the very stupid mustache I'm currently cultivating—to small ones, like chatting with strangers on street corners. I acquired a truly terrible cat, a rather shitty apartment, and quite a few tattoos.

One of the stranger parts of my journey has been a return to faith. I'm back at the church I grew up in, a small, progressive Baptist church. It's full of other queers and sweet old folks who are absolute champs about my pronouns. Many of them have known me since before I was born. We just hosted our second annual drag fundraiser for PFLAG. I'd call it a second family, but with my mother there as well, I think it may just be "family."

I don't think about my marriage daily anymore, but I'm also not over it. The guilt remains, as does the regret. I think I can now say that I feel less guilt about the divorce than I do about having gotten married in the first place, when I knew, quite clearly, that I didn't want it. It feels like I lied for all thirteen years of marriage—like I took away not only my own chances of happiness, but his as well. People like to remind me that I was afraid, as if this absolves me of blame, as if absolution is what I need. It's difficult to explain that I need the guilt in some strange way, because guilt implies agency, and it has been a long, hard journey to believe that I have the ability to make my own choices. If I want to believe that I can make good choices for myself, for the people I love, then I also need to believe I can make bad ones.

New Orleans is a city shaped by precarity, in a state that would happily legislate me out of existence. As I write this, we're sitting at the beginning of hurricane season and gearing up for an absolutely terrifying election. I'm afraid. I don't know any trans people who aren't. I used to have security, of a sort. I had a husband and a house in the suburbs and a savings account. I gave up those things in the divorce; and although my bank account may not reflect it, I am infinitely richer than I was before. For the first time in my adult life, I have a future that I am afraid of losing, which is both terrifying and wonderful. I may be objectively less safe now, but I am myself, and I am free.

Thirty-Six to One Year

MARINA MONTES DE OCA

A month after I discovered Ramsay's affair and asked them to leave the home we shared as a family with our son, I downloaded my first dating app. Despite both of us making wild threats and unrealistic demands over custody in those first few tenuous weeks of separation, we managed to agree on a time-share plan that liberated me from full-time childcare on some weekends—a luxury I hadn't enjoyed since my kid was born nine years ago. I sat at home alone on one of these Fridays, smoking pot *inside* the house, free from the buzzing sound of video games and cartoons that normally took up the space around me, feeling especially thoughtful and overly confident, and made calculations of how many people I thought I could sleep with in the span of a year. At the time, I had been off the market for over a decade and was eager to get back to casual dating, so I set the bar just below high, coming to a number that I could have certainly accomplished in my most promiscuous days before marriage. If I slept with three different people a month, I could get to thirty-six by the time I naively projected my divorce would be final. I had persuaded myself into believing I was pretty good at doing marriage; but when that failed, I knew I was great at doing dating.

My besties helped me create profiles on the apps that were most popular in the queer dating scene, some of which sounded familiar since I'd heard about them in passing conversations with my single and poly friends and acquaintances. We uploaded pictures of me from their phones: me in a retro two-piece from girls' weekend at Joshua Tree; me after I cut my hair short and dyed it pink as a show of rebellion against the expectations of beauty that had been imposed upon me in my marriage; me at brunch in Mid-City with a mimosa in my hand; me pointing to poster art with suggestively graphic text. I answered cliché prompts with charming responses, added cute stickers to the bottoms of the pages ("Pillow Princess" in pink cursive with a little bejeweled crown emblem—adorable), and searched the internet for all the new terms and multiple sets of identities that were not around when I last created an online dating account on OkCupid. The box I had once clicked for "lipstick lesbian" in the early 2000s was gone now and had been replaced with "femme/top from the bottom." Check.

As soon as my profile became viewable, my notification bar started to ping with likes, hearts, and emojis. After going through a selection process where I considered physical attractiveness, geographic desirability, and sexual preferences, I responded to one of the likes with the first direct message I would send on the apps. "Do you want a play date?" On the other end was a stunning leather stud that used "ze/zir" pronouns and went by the name "Six." Zir profile had several selfies, but the hottest one was a close-up of zir ornate chest tattoo peeping through a studded vintage motorcycle club vest. It was hard to tell if ze was trying to be ironic in zir representation of '90s lesbian subculture, or if this look authentically captured zir true personal style. On recommendation from my best gay advisor, I set up an introductory phone call to prove I was a real human and to screen for any hints of mental instability. He also urged me to hide my laptop and other impulse items that an opportunistic lover may find too enticing to leave behind, if I ever brought anyone back to my place.

Six suggested a club in Long Beach for "Latin" girls' night for our date—my first one in fourteen years. We both showed up at the same time and somehow managed to park side by side in the lot adjacent to the building. We recognized each other from our online pics and started making out before saying hello. Once inside the venue, we sat near the dance floor watching curvy strippers on short portable platforms bouncing up and down in mesmerizing rhythms to the energetic pulse of salsa. I tried making small talk and learned that ze was staying at a hotel near downtown and had moved to LA after getting "too involved" in the gang scene back in zir hometown of Detroit. As it turned out, we didn't have much in common. What we did have was an immediate physical attraction that took us from groping in a dark corner booth at the club to my house for the first one-night stand I would have in a series of one-nighters that followed. Before we entered my home, while we were standing at the front doorway, I revealed in a quick, nonchalant statement that I had a son and his toys were all over the living room (so please be careful where you walk). Six didn't seem to mind that I was a mom or that I had kept that piece of my life hidden; ze was already stepping over Transformers, eager to reach my bedroom. Ze continued to grab my tits and ass as I backed away and walked toward the kitchen, stopping at the fridge to politely offer an alcoholic beverage. I was drinking a lot those days on all the noncustodial nights, so I had a diverse selection to present. Beers, cocktails in a can, hard stuff meant to be poured over ice even though I never did, and several sweet mixers. Ze scoffed menacingly, looked over my shoulder at the food on the shelves and said, "Make me a bagel," (bitch) . . . so I complied.

And then we fucked. Zir skin was smooth like the most polished stone, but zir hands were rough and aggressive—pushing, pulling, and penetrating my body with zir slick black cock. Each thrust of zir hips pushed a door from shut to wide open; on the other side was the freedom to want again that had lain dormant. My desire unlocked, aroused in a familiar way that reminded me of the excitement that came from my first sexual encounters as a teenager, when I got to live out my gay fantasies. Here I was experiencing the stirring for a second time. I had given up on bodily pleasure years ago, had stopped finding my spouse attractive, and could not remember the last time I masturbated. Intercourse had become routine, a mechanical version of the sex we'd shared as lovers in the before times. My entire purpose had evolved into playing the role of ideal mother and spouse, and sexuality became unnecessary in that pursuit. The moment I accepted my marriage was over, the healing started, and with the first step out came an intense desire for sexual gratification. My pussy was wet all day, growing more ravenous with each tiny bite from a willing player. The barista with the ear plugs at the Starbucks drive-through; the young guy at El Super who spoke to me in Spanish and asked me how my day was but didn't have to; the dyke with the neck tattoo delivering my FedEx packages; and every unattached and almost unattached dad that I came across: all of them were game, all getting the flirty, sparkly version of myself that thrived in the days before sexual bankruptcy.

After hours of sex, Six stood up next to my bed, very close to my face, moved zir fingers down the strap of zir harness to release the belt loops, pushed the dildo to one side, and begged me to touch zir enormous clit. I looked up at the curl of zir lip that was both perverse and adorable as ze gently brushed the strands of my hair back, stared into zir midnight-infinity-pool eyes, and said, "No way!" I was not feeling reciprocal. That wasn't the intent I had for our date. My body was hollow, and filling it became my focus; so I offered a blow job instead. I rolled the condom off, putting zir tip in my mouth while my tongue moved in circular motions, stopped and whispered, "Your cock is so beautiful," before bringing the seven inches of silicone so deeply into the back of my throat I couldn't breathe. Ze cupped the back of my head, violently pressing me towards zir crotch until I felt full, and ze came. I was at capacity.

In those first few weeks of discovery after confirming my spouse's long-term infidelity, I didn't allow myself any sense of gratification; my stomach remained mostly empty for days, where nothing more than pomegranate seeds took up space. I had no appetite for food or sleep, running on reserves for the stamina needed to reflect on the last two years of our life together. As I scrolled through (excess) amounts of messages on our family plan's phone records and dissected every transaction on our joint bank account (Did they buy a candlelight concert while lying in bed recovering from top surgery? How much did they spend at the sex shop?), I was left depleted and thirsty for answers. I scrutinized my calendar, taking note of every work-related conference trip they took, a late night they said was spent hospitalizing a client, and every family event they found excuses to miss. The deception was all there, buried shallowly and poorly disguised, quietly waiting beneath the surface to be easily excavated. Probing gave me a focus, a distraction from meeting the needs of my neglected body.

Instead of investigating during the prior year when my instincts hinted that something was off, I had chosen to ignore the inner voice that had served me so well in motherhood and trusted that my spouse would never jeopardize what we had worked for years to create. I had sold the idea of a queer marriage to my traditional, first-generation Mexican family, asking them to welcome my white spouse as a permanent member of our tight-knit clan. When I became pregnant again after miscarrying our first conception, my family was thrilled. They related to our choices as a couple, legitimizing our marriage with their sense of familiarity. I was performing the mother and wife script the way I had been groomed to believe would result in acceptance and love from the hetero world around me. And when I felt pangs of unhappiness land nearby, I simply walked over them so we could continue to participate in the privileges that straight couples were awarded, so we could have a long future as a family unit. So I could show my son what it meant to come from a home where both parents still respected and liked each other. I didn't realize what I was sacrificing.

The day Ramsay moved all their belongings out of our house, I stayed as far away as I could. When I got home that night, I walked over to the highboy that had once held their clothes. My mom had painted the dresser an opaque slate blue and replaced the original knobs with ornate brass pulls as a nursery gift when Emerson was born. Somehow it migrated to the corner of our bedroom and by default became my spouse's. I looked inside, preparing myself for the vacant space I expected. Instead, I saw the only two things that were left behind: two cocks. Prepregnancy and postpregnancy dildos rocking back and forth in unison, animated by the clumsy movement of the secondhand drawer, bobbing from one rubber vein to the other like buoys in water. I feverishly pulled every drawer open looking for the strap, but it was gone. I was in a frenzy, whipping through the house looking for any possessions of theirs I could find, intent on removing their presence from the space we'd once occupied together. I quickly walked over to the garage. Ramsay had asked if they could store a few things there until they found a more permanent place to live. I found a hamper with clothes haphazardly stacked on top of each other in a messy pile. Sitting on top was a leather jacket I was led to believe was a gift from their boss during a work trip to Boston. I was skeptical at the time, as it seemed too generous a gesture from a professional colleague, but I never questioned it; I submitted and moved on. But here I was, on the other side of infidelity, feeling more and more in control of my surrounding space. After looking through every zipped pocket in case there was cash to keep or evidence to burn, I threw the jacket in the trash.

Two months into separation, I hooked up with Six and the searching persisted. I found myself starting to digest the divorce more rapidly, feeding on sex to provide me with nourishment and healing. Six left my house early the next morning, and other than a text message thanking me for a "fun" night, we never communicated again. I continued chatting with other potentials online, swiping right and down to set up dates for the following weekends. Despite an earnest commitment to the plan, I didn't end up reaching my goal. Coparenting, being a single mom, and engaging with my ex-spouse did not get easier with the salve of a thirty-six-cock project. In fact, nothing about divorce got easier to navigate; however, I did sense a notable shift after that first one-night stand. With the help of just a handful of blow jobs I was able to retrace my steps back to a period long gone, a time when my purpose seemed the clearest, when I felt invincible, and when pleasure, whimsy, freedom, and queerness were central to my existence. A young past, before the pressure to follow life's prescribed playbook took precedence over the quest for real joy. The lubed-up dildos and penetrating fingers of strangers filling my mouth and pussy made me feel like the fleshy walls behind my skin would split open and break if I inhaled too deeply; I'd hold my breath and wait to feel whole. Cumming magically drew a path leading toward the time-machine portal where I could enter a world of youthful liberty and sanctioned love.

I started to realize all the ways in which my marriage had denied me that life, and I was elated to be given an opportunity for rebirth. The hunger for sex never subsided. I masturbated so much that if anyone glanced at my phone, they would see that three out of the top five most-frequented sites on my browser were devoted to adult content. An inviting smile from the delivery driver at work as they asked for my signature kept me wet all day. And my secret fantasies of taking them to the back room for a quickie kept me going until the next day when more packages would arrive. Eventually my cravings for promiscuity and anonymous sex began to wane. The dating apps went neglected and I deactivated my accounts, and a year after my spouse stepped away from our marriage and their affair was exposed, I was moving on. I felt alive, complete.

Open in Case of Emergency

ALEKS LIOU

on the day you get divorced
you dance on top of a mountain to "best of my love" by the emotions
the wind and the ocean greet you like celebratory friends
they fill your lungs with the force of freedom
"congratulations!" say the foxtails and ravens—
swaying and squawking with glee—
you grew to love yourself so deeply
become secure in your own magic
you realized *i was my own soulmate all along*
& if i needed to be ruptured to experience
surrender
divinity
rapture
then i thank her for taking the sword to my throat
i never would have had the courage to jump into oblivion
but now i'd do it all over again,
die a dozen more deaths to experience myself unconditionally
it's priceless to be able to tell you now
baby,
you were happy when you got married
and you were happier when you got divorced

Well here we are. In sunny California, like we've always wanted. For the first time in my adult life, I feel free. Just completely capable of walking whichever way I want to, in whatever direction is available to me, with the multitude of unfolding paths just pulsating right in front of me. I just want me. I want to chase my sparkle and my glow. I feel like this life is rife with experiences that are waiting to change me, love me, welcome me, call me home, call me into spaces and community and people who can and are ready to change me. Seems almost like a blessing that I got hurt (is that just what we tell ourselves when we're too hurt?), but it's opened me up to really think about what I want out of my one precious, sacred, little, mighty, beautiful life.

I remember learning when Mom passed away that we walk into and out of this world alone. I mean, there are our loved ones waiting for us on both sides of the plane, the space-time continuum, but walking across/through the portal? That's something only we can do ourselves. We have to do ourselves. And I feel so blessed that that death taught me how to grieve, so I know how to get through this death now. To trust myself. To be the partner and parent and friend that I'll need throughout my life, and especially when my time comes, to know that my existence is/was a gift and that I gave and received those gifts so generously. I've learned detachment and healthy attachment (not completely, but kind of), and I find myself right now entering the next cycle of my life knowing I can move into and out of relations with people, places, and things, where control, anxiety, and fear of them leaving me won't devastate me. I lost Mom, I lost my first love, and now I'm wiser and more in tune with myself. I know what the taste of individuality and self-determination and autonomy look like, what trust in myself feels like, what kind of doors it opens up, what kind of people that attracts into my life. I know the feelings I want to keep close in my life, the plants I want to water, the relationships I want to nurture and tend to—the most important of them being my relationship to myself.

I want to walk into the next phase of my life knowing that every divine possibility out there is mine. Every fantasy I've ever had, every wild dream I've wanted to chase, everything I've wanted to learn, every love I've been curious to taste, is out there for me. I want to be gentle with myself, patient, and give myself time to figure it all out and make things beautiful. I want to be the partner I deserve, I want to woo myself, I want to spoil myself with pleasure and romance and desire, and I want to feel truly safe in my own presence. I want to make my life an altar to the ancestors, to myself; I want to make us proud of what I do with my autonomy. As an offering. Wow, I came here to experience life and bounty and love and liberation, and may my whole life be a testament, a testimony, living proof that this life is nothing if not good and possible and sweet and precious, gracious, even what hurts and what's ugly is divine. A beautiful life is not a clean, neat, or linear one, one with all the answers, the one that others told me to want. A beautiful life is one where you can tell stories that start with, "I was scared to do it, but I did it anyway and met myself more deeply because of it."

Losing something clears the way for new love and possibility to grow. After I made peace with grief after losing Mom, new parts of me became possible for myself. I don't know if I would have felt the freedom to reinvent and follow my instincts, change my name, take testosterone, walk in the direction of direct action and fearlessness, if I hadn't first lost everything I was scared of losing. I never wanted to lose Mom, so I would have lived my whole life so as to keep her. To not upset her. I would have done it willingly and happily, but I might not have ever arrived at a relationship with myself, the one I have now. I know that Mom is happy for me to have taken such deep pain and sorrow and transformed it into self-love. I know she sees me better now, in this version of myself, than she did in the version of myself I was able to share with her. I know she bears witness to this version of me too.

The pain of moving on, letting go, is really hard. Because there is a lot of pleasure in comfort and routine, the safety of the known. And it's overwhelming to think there is so much you'll need to let go of in order to take on the next iteration of yourself. Letting go of the future you thought you'd have, the pureness of your trust and love before they got broken. Nowadays, I'm more afraid of the difficulty of living a life where I have to compromise myself and my desires, my idea of what's beautiful, for the rest of my life. I fear I'll look back on this pivotal juncture in my life and see that I shrank myself to fit somewhere, that I spent time fixing what I didn't break, that I looked at the shortchanging of myself as an opportunity to prove my worth to someone who took me for granted. We tell each other that we have to honor our commitments, and I'm not someone to go back on my word, but I'm also not someone who thinks lukewarm honoring is the right way to live. I only want things for myself that I enthusiastically, hungrily consent to. I don't want to betray myself anymore.

I want to run—sprint—unabashedly in the direction of my dreams. My destiny in this life is to do what makes me come alive. I want to practice Buddhism and mindfulness more, I want to eat less meat (maybe none at all), I want to go to Taiwan and reconnect with my culture and heritage. I want to stretch myself into the spirit I was meant to be, I want to keep metamorphosing, shape-shifting, growing, I want to keep unfolding and expanding to the point where the universe and god and buddhas and the ancestors need to keep repotting me—because there's not a pot big enough for me, til the day I return to the earth.

I don't want to take things personally anymore. Everyone around me is going through their own version of transformation. Transforming, transfiguring—those things are really messy and imperfect processes. I don't need to be hurt by what other people are doing; I only need to hurt when I notice myself betraying or abandoning myself to accommodate the pressures around me. I want to get over myself. I want to tuck away my ego and tell it to take a nap.

My ideas of love and partnership and family have changed so much in the last six months. I see what love rooted in respect, joy, and reciprocity looks like. All around that witnessing, my ex mirrored to me what I once thought it was: devotion, sacrifice, control, jealousy, anger, volatility, intense emotions, unconditionality, the melding of selves. I might just experience pleasure in my physical body for now, but I know what I really crave is an equal. I want to be understood, respected, valued, and safe. I want to know what it's like to breathe and laugh when I receive love as pure and gentle and generous as I give it. I know it will find me. The universe wants it to.

Everyone tells me it's time. I'm generally an anxious overprepper. But this time, I trust what I have on my person, within my heart, and my own two feet to get me there. No more waiting for her to catch up, to learn how, to figure it out, to process. I'm going now. I'm on my way, and I'm not looking back. My future is mine, and it's up to me.

Shattered

DOMINIKA BEDNARSKA

I wasn't aware you could actually physically feel your heart shattering, as though someone stabbed you. It's one of those things you don't have reason to think about until it happens. I'm not really sure why. I was worried about so many things, but I never considered the pain of feeling that moment. I was worried about rent, homelessness, illness (yours or mine), retirement, how we would support ourselves when our bodies or capitalism inevitability failed us. But my only heart shattering like a cheap plate was not a real concern.

For some time after you left, I thought I would wake up and find you there and tell you about the crazy dream I had where you left and I fell out of my wheelchair and into the bus lane on Market Street and I sprained a finger, possibly permanently, and my dad came to stay with me and made all this terrible food and burned everything and then you would cuddle and reassure me and make breakfast.

My heart is in a locked steel box underneath my bed and pushed so far back behind other things, like the rope you once tied me up with, that I won't be able to get to it anymore anyway.

We lived in this apartment for seven years and we never cleaned out the second bedroom. You shoved random things in boxes and then left in less than three days. I don't recall you showing that kind of initiative with anything else around the house.

I've lost my mind. Should I pay someone to cast a spell so you will come home? When my mind comes back she is going to be pissed.

You used my disability, ableism, and my deepest wound against me so you wouldn't have to own your pain. Neither my body, nor my life, nor my love were something that happened to you. You signed up for this and promised forever—by which you meant for now?

I think of the kind words I said to you and smile. How we would fetch each other with "kitten." I can hear you apologizing to me and crying, saying, "I did not want to break up, I just didn't know what else to do." You still responded to Lovie and the million other nicknames we had for each other. You are still sitting somewhere, thinking of me, staring at my books that you won't return.

I remember when we started dating. You said, "I'm glad to see your books." I once dated a girl who had no books in her apartment. It made me so suspicious. I had to ask, "Where are your books?"

And then, years later, you would take my books without asking, with no discussion. The bookshelf is see-through and bare.

I started watching videos on twin flames like soulmates that say things like, "You are the same soul so you start to repel each other. If you just change your energy and pull it back she will come back. Just visualize. Just write out limiting beliefs." I am offered coaching for $3,500, and I stop watching videos about twin flames. It boiled down to "be confident and she will be back." Or, you know, she *won't*. If someone wants to be with you, they will.

I was at a party, and a woman said the same thing happened to her and it gets better. She said, "I've accepted that I am going to spend the next twenty years processing this." She was now poly, and I watched her get tied up in a position that would be too uncomfortable for me to hold. Her lover teases her about how hard it is to balance. I've played too, but it feels insignificant. I know my wife would never come to a party like this. I miss her and want to go home.

My father has come to stay with me until I can get other help. He is mostly depressed and obnoxious. I am angry that he is not my wife and that he is not any more patient or compassionate than when he was an active alcoholic. We are both terrible to each other. We are both trying, sort of. We both kind of hate each other and we both stay. My marriage had better food. My mother is mostly worried about his depression. She wants him to come home. Sometimes he just goes to bed. I haven't eaten dinner in weeks now. He stopped offering and I stopped asking.

The last night we spent together, I asked for some food, and you gave me chicken heated in the microwave for too long. Finally, I could taste the resentment that came out in quick, hot bursts, followed by disavowal. Like the beep of the microwave, it was quick and it was over.

You have sent me a couple of emails about PG&E bills and ignored my emails about my belongings. You haven't written at all in almost a month. People say "there is something we don't know," which is code for "she is having an affair." I offered to open up the relationship, and you looked crushed and pained, but what do I know? Clearly not you.

There are power outages throughout the state. I have power but am working twelve-hour days on behalf of disabled people who don't. We don't have the resources. Every reasonable plan or idea I have is shot down. I am talked over repeatedly and shushed. I am the only disabled person in the room. The city tells disabled people to "use their own resources and not depend on city emergency services." There is a fire on Twitter in response. The angry posts from disabled people explode. I call people and they are angry and I am too. We don't have the budget to help anyone in the way they deserve.

Instead of offering them a place to stay, I tell them to call 911. I am embarrassed, but I need my job now. Able-bodied men already complained that I was too assertive. My coworkers think it is a "great learning experience."

When my mind wanders, I think of trips we took together: Los Angeles, the Netherlands, Hawaii. Even when ableism made things shitty, we still had fun, didn't we? I have to step outside at lunch to cry. I called my mother, and she said I should try calling someone.

"But I just called you," I said.

Sunday hits me like some kind of meteor. I call my friend, and she says PG&E keeps coming up. It seems like this is all about power. She does not live in California. Still, I've stopped believing that things can ever be equal. That idea feels like a mirage—like adequate budgets for access.

You took a hundred books with you, at least. This included mainly queer theory but also disability books, novels, and poems too. You took my copy of *Exile and Pride*, written by Eli Clare, a transgender disabled writer who was one of the very first disabled queer people I ever met. It was a first edition, bought just months after it was first published. I heard him read it at my college LGBT Center and every part of my body vibrated with the fear and excitement that comes with self-recognition. It was worn, annotated with three different highlighters, and signed by Clare for me. I mumbled something, and he said, "Feel free to call me, because you seem so isolated here," and I was and I read that book and I had a language. I read and read it and cried and cried. I thought maybe there are others. Maybe there is hope. Sometimes I want to write to you again and say, "Can I just have the Clare back?" That would make a difference.

I am extroverted. I survive by reaching out to friends and by meeting new people. I went on OkCupid and sent some messages. I got a response from someone who was persistent, and that I didn't mind. We went out a few times, and eventually I took breaks from wondering when you would write me. She only just kissed me the other night and is already worried that I will be hurt.

She is dating many people and has no time, at least none that she wants to promise to me with any regularity.

"You are already so hurt," she said. "I don't want to hurt you more."

"I am not looking for a rescue," I said. "Just like we have learned in emergency preparedness, no one is coming, and you have to save yourself."

"Oh no," she replies, half-laughing, but it's true, no one is coming.

The next day her girlfriend's house likely burns in a fire. She evacuated so we can't be sure yet. Another partner of hers works for PG&E.

I keep thinking these past few days about when we first started dating and how you said you were in love with me, first, so early, and you were crushed when I didn't say it back right away. I was never one to fall quickly, ever. My heart was padded over with years of unearned rejections, based mostly on people's fears and the ease of moving on. I tried to explain that I needed time, but you heard rejection. Weeks later, I told you I loved you too. When I broached the subject of moving in together, something I had never done before, despite some valiant efforts on the part of my ex-girlfriends, you said, "It's okay, it's okay, you can ask. I want to live with you and I want to marry you."

"That's ridiculous," I said, "it's too soon."

I remember the first time you asked me to marry you. You said "give me your hand," and you put on my finger a very oversized ring that fell off. I thought you were making fun of me for wanting to marry you. We exchanged that ring for one with a pearl because it reminded me of your name. Rings are hard for me to wear for practical reasons, but I liked to wear it when I had something stressful to do, because it reminded me of you and it made me feel peaceful. I think I told this to Melissa, the woman who cleans my teeth, because I remember her saying that's how you know you've chosen the right one. Yes. I agreed.

When we met, you mentioned reading a queer theory book that I wrote about in my dissertation. You are not an academic and that was really impressive. We hear Cornel West speak and it's great, but you are also super critical and I agree with all parts of it. I am impressed by your mind. Another night you tell me that I am very comfortable with myself and that is very attractive. I start really paying attention to you, like you might be here for me, you might really see me. It's rarer than one might think. In my case, it seems to have taken thirty-one years.

Toward the end, you kept saying, "We aren't equals in this relationship."

My therapist said your lack of response regarding my things, recipes, and paperwork is all about power.

I said, "But she has all the power." She responded, "Yes, but that is not her perception."

You never talked about your first wife. We had an argument because you waited so long to mention her and by then we spent so much time together and you knew so much about me. We agreed on no more secrets, but you could not keep that promise. Years later you would get an apartment behind my back, keeping it secret for weeks, and leave me in three days' time. You promised you would never leave me like the several disabled friends I know whose spouses have left them. The day before you told me you were leaving, you reassured me that we would be okay. It always worried me, the way you never talked about your first wife, like she never existed. It scared me that you would do the same thing to me. "No," you said, "it's just painful to talk about." We got married. The years went by. I let it go.

My dad really wants to leave now. We both know it isn't working and I am begging him not to abandon me. If it's not a perfect parallel for my marriage, what is? Getting hit by a bus? Running from a wildfire? Dying in the dark due to lack of power? Some things are too big to compare to anything else.

Postscript: I wrote this essay over five years ago, in the first few weeks after my wife left me. It is so raw and vulnerable for me that I thought about publishing this under a pseudonym. However, I decided not to because I've learned in the years since that while being "discarded" in this way is not typical, it does happen to people and it's perhaps more common than one would think. This knowledge helped me heal and better understand what happened to me. As with any kind of trauma, internalizing the simple truth that we are not responsible for other people's actions or decisions or trauma, only our own, brought me great comfort. If you are going through or have gone through a similar experience, I hope it does the same for you. I also want to say that my life is more stable now. I have all the logistical support I need. Up until Trump got elected, I had meaningful work. I have friends and all types of family. My wife leaving was the worst thing that ever happened to me, but not the most defining thing.

Close Separation—Our Love Beyond Marriage

W. E. CUTHBERT

We both spent our wedding day dissociated.

It wasn't the fairytale I'd expected or longed for since being a little girl fantasizing about *The One*—who *he* would be. And it was always "him" I imagined, in the Disney princess days of my girlhood.

I hadn't imagined the anticipation of the ceremony would feel so lonely in my white gown, in the grey light of an overcast early spring day, just my sister sitting next to me on the hotel bed.

I'd never thought about the requirement to spend the day being a spectacle for guests, making our relationship a public performance.

I can count away the layers of our routine, portraying other people.

Spending inheritance money, family money, little of it our own earnings, on something we convinced ourselves was worth it.

In each other's arms, tulle-sheathed satin twisted around my ankles, misunderstanding ourselves.

Everything calmed and solidified, my sense of time coming back to me, when we could lie in the bridal suite alone together.

But to this day, I still go stiff with alarm when I remember my stepfather slept, by sheer coincidence, on the other side of the wall from our bed.

That man, the one who walked me down the aisle, would disown me three years and two weeks later. Not even this could deepen the preexisting wounds of his emotional and sexual abuse, or my intuition that he wouldn't make room in his new life, with a new partner, for a trans stepchild by his dead wife.

Unembraced and ghosted by extended family, marriage identified me to my supposed husband, and them to me, as all the things we pretended to be to get by—a working man and the stay-at-home mum, visiting the in-laws on weekends.

We're autistic and ADHD, both polyamorous and on the asexual/aromantic spectrum. Both transgender. Neither of us fully realized or accepted any of these things when we married.

For years, because we don't always feel romantic toward one another, we believed something to be wrong with "us." We'd grow emotionally distant, then back together in our own patterns, passing through times that felt like the end, unable to comprehend that these may have been organic movements of our love.

I came out as trans in 2021. We'd been together for nine years, but only married for two. This time of powerful self-realization sparked months of falling in love anew after the rift of an abortion and the long depression that left me crumpled on the bathroom floor on New Year's Day that same year.

But we would always seem to fall apart again.

Even as we began to grasp our neurodivergence in our separate spheres, through my partner coming out as trans in 2023, and all the renewed strength and closeness that came with those realizations, the shared sense that we didn't feel right punctured back through.

It came around to arguments again. About my failings to show them the affection they needed, our lack of disposable income to live the way we wanted, and how it could all be different if I'd "just get a job." These themes would recur and interweave almost every time we had it out.

It's the nature of these arguments that their details and how they started are forgotten. But one of them led to my partner saying that perhaps we'd make more sense as friends.

I agreed. It defused the fight. I took that as the proof we were better apart.

I made plans to move out. We told our six-year-old it was going to happen. We packed my books into boxes, started buying doubles of store cupboard foods to start me off in a place of my own, on my own.

It would have been my first time living independently. The cushion of university only ever provided an illusion of true agency. I wanted the time and space living alone could offer me to do my writing and exist on my own terms as someone who worked to support myself.

I wanted to make my own friends IRL without feeling like I was always hanging off a partner's arm. I'd been ready to find new love for years, to explore the freshly unearthed territory of my polyamory.

When we decided to separate, these wants of mine had gone against their needs for a consistent lifestyle and sole devotion in love.

I wanted to leave for the freedom, not to be without them.

I hadn't planned to mirror my biological father by abandoning my child. Giving her the advance warning I never got, after all, didn't change the outcome.

In my journal one night, I'd spill my worries about the sense that I'd already abandoned her as a mother and now meant to push her away even further.

Family ties are still strangled by trauma. My second chance at having a dad ended when my stepfather first groped my chest as a young teen, my mother an apologist for his actions: "It's just what men do when they're drunk."

I heard those words of hers through auditory fog, unable to see or speak to defend myself, even if I'd known how.

This response arose from trauma-activated autistic shutdown. Not that I had the tools to know this until I began to find them myself, at the age of thirty after three years of marriage, with my four-year-old relying on me to learn fast.

I don't know if I'm experienced enough with healthy, interdependent love, from parents or knowing men my mother married, to be reliable as a partner or a parent.

Yet, for removing the invisible pressure of the expectations that come with married life from our daily togetherness, my partner has seen my attitude as a parent soften in ways I hadn't noticed myself. I'm becoming a gentler, less tense carer, less prone to snapping at her for silly reasons.

I'd been prepared to let them both go. Now it's easier to see where I took them for granted, and to work harder not to.

The morning after that journal entry, all I wanted when I got up was to go back to bed with my ex-partner. I told them this, not knowing if it was right to want. "Okay," they said, and went to tell work that they wouldn't be in.

As they turned the corner from the kitchen, I sobbed a few quiet times in relief, in happy disbelief that at last, I had someone who would support me this way. They accept parts of me I once thought would never be nourished by unconditional tenderness. My traumatized inability to be degraded by nine-to-five working life, held together by them.

We still always shared a bed while separating. Kissing and making love, in a long goodbye we worked on forgiveness, checking old patterns of self-pitying and suffering in silence, communicating our needs. Being better friends.

For me, it was my first time meeting them beyond wedded borders, as I'd always expected to marry *The One*, once I found whoever that could be.

Unmarried from each other, we fell deeper in love.

Now we're healing from the damage of the cishetero marriage structure we'd felt expected to inhabit in bliss, our kid completing the cake-topper set.

I'm educating myself in what it takes to show love despite childhood and family trauma, as a disabled nonbinary queer who loves a neurodivergent trans lesbian.

We're imagining a future polycule. It's given us practice in setting out our boundaries, talking about what's important to us, both together and as independently thinking and feeling beings.

We had none of this language, whether for closeness or respecting our individual autonomy, between first meeting in the twilight of our teens and almost ending.

It's been a matter of months since the argument that divided us the way we needed and helped us move past our resentments as presumed married people, almost from the moment I read their love poems for me.

Without unmarrying, we would still be blaming each other for the wrongness our world insisted we perform.

We won't be going through the legal process of divorce—certainly not yet, or in any great hurry. For the sake of our family as it looks today, it's easier and safer to keep our marital privilege.

Our romance isn't constant, but we still hold out love for each other and the hypothetical third person we might find in time.

Our feelings will continue to change. But I doubt knowing that will ever amount to us not adoring one another, exactly as we are.

The Reckoning

JANIS VOGEL

I am getting divorced. The divorce process starts today. Today is a beginning of the end. A severing of ties.

I have been reckoning.

I have reckoned with ending my marriage.

I have reckoned with how to write.

I have been waiting to write until the reckoning crystallizes into an answer I can share.

The answers are not coming. I cannot wait for gems. Please sift through sand with me.

I have reckoned with how to write about my relationship (without harming anyone, especially my child, but also my ex). I have reckoned with how to write about childhood (without shaming anyone).

I have reckoned with how to write about myself while the world is burning.

I have reckoned with how to write about toxicity without being depressing and cleansing without being pretentious, about abuse without being dark, about luck without seeming privileged, about the dear universe without undermining harsh reality.

The truth is . . . my truth. I will seem, and must risk seeming, to harvest the gold of being. To reap the gift of resonating with my people, I must risk "seeming" to those who are not . . . my people. I must risk rupture anew, knowing those who love me will be willing to repair.

I must risk writing something I regret, and then writing about the fallout, and then writing about the repair, and writing about the new perspective I have gained.

Writing feels so final, but it's just the center of the process for some of us. I don't write to set things in stone; I write to move a river through me.

The truth is, there's no controlling the narrative. And that is scary, but holding on to the narrative, hiding it, is painful.

The proof is in the pain pudding.

My lower back aches, and the more I write about that, the more it aches, as if, after being acknowledged, it can finally share its full pain.

I reckoned with whether to leave.

I reckoned with my child's heart.

I reckoned with choices where both paths were heartbreaking.

For my child to see a relationship I wouldn't wish upon her.

Or for my child to see me half the time.

To miss half my child's life.

Or to miss my own life.

I reckoned with my future, my imagined happy ending.

I reckoned with breaking the cycle.

When my marriage began falling apart, I doubled down in my determination to keep it together. I poured my soul's glue into holding the family unit together, in the name of breaking the cycle. I thought breaking the cycle meant giving my child the nuclear family trajectory I didn't have.

I did everything I could, everything in my exhausted power, to put out the fires, replant loving seeds, and heal together.

A tiny part of me. Seven-year-old me, who loved workbooks, and filling out sweepstakes forms just for the satisfaction of filling all the blanks. Miss Janis Vogel could ask, "But did you try this?" again and again forever.

She is so determined.

Be careful what fights you are determined to win, what races you sign up for, who you make it your mission to prove yourself to. That is my note to her.

I reckoned with permission. I wanted the leaving to be as mutual as the love at first sight. We hugged on our first date and it felt so right.

I reckon with permission now to write this, to reveal this. My stomach turns.

These words are mine. They aren't the whole truth; they are my truth.

I reckoned with failure.

I reckoned with being sure.

I reckoned with chances.

I reckoned with giving up and giving up *on*.

I reckoned with abandonment and abandoning.

I reckoned with fear of financial ruin and ruining.

I reckoned with not being perfect.

I reckoned with punishing when I wasn't innocent.

I reckoned with taking off my wedding ring.

I reckoned with how we built a life against all odds, and how I'd have to rebuild my own against more.

I reckoned with fear of the dark.

I reckoned with being alone.

I reckoned with leaping into the unknown.

The greatest lesson in all of this has been learning that to be caught, you must leap.

To let go of his hand, I held many others, and my own.

One by one, my friends, my family, my therapist, my coaches, and my communities vowed to catch me.

Here I am at dawn, in my own apartment. My child still asleep at her father's house.

Turns out the dark is just the dark.

From the Old Hope to the New Life

KIRA RY

Hope. Disappointment. Despair. Pain. New life.

These words perfectly describe my marriage, my divorce, and how my life changed after transitioning from male to female. It moved in a sine wave pattern with ups replacing downs, and back and forth.

My name is Kira, and I'm a transgender woman who began transitioning a year ago, in my early thirties. It took six months from the day I realized I was transgender—in other words, when my "egg cracked"—to the day I separated from my ex-wife. Our marriage lasted for ten years, during which we had two amazing sons, both kind, intelligent, and open-minded.

During those ten years, we both changed, each in our own way. Today, we wouldn't recognize our old selves; the people who decided to marry no longer exist.

I was born in a male body, raised by my mom to be a "true man," as she loved to say, and followed all the social norms expected of men. My first signs of dysphoria were noticeable by the age of four and persisted throughout my life. Conservative attitudes and societal pressures suppressed these feelings. In my childhood, it was shameful to be different. The worst insults were "you're not a man" or "you're one of those," meaning a member of the LGBTQ+ community. In my case, it was true, but such words never really caused internal conflict. However, I hid my truth out of fear of social shame.

My ex-wife was also raised with conservative beliefs: Men worked, and women kept the house and raised kids. Topics like identity, gender roles, and equality were never discussed and were seen as unnecessary, invented ideas spread by propaganda.

Neither of us questioned whether we were okay with these norms because that was just how things worked. In our view, any deviation would damage the delicate mechanism of life, and everything would fall apart. We met at university, moved in together after two months, and married one and a half years later, shortly after a positive pregnancy test.

I was present during the delivery of our first son, and it was a moment of true contentment. Due to health issues, my ex-wife couldn't breastfeed, so we bottle-fed him, taking turns and sharing responsibilities. Despite the sleepless nights and extra stress, I felt real maternal instincts. Of course, at the time, I refused to acknowledge it when people said I acted like a mother with her child. That idea didn't fit into my worldview.

We built our family in an unhealthy way from the very beginning. It was rooted in mutual codependency, which made our separation far more painful and difficult. I depended on her for emotional validation, constant praise, support for every step I took, and housekeeping. She depended on me financially and relied on me to make every decision, solve every problem, and take responsibility for our family's actions. We weren't interchangeable. Looking back, I see this as a mistake. At the time, though, we didn't ask ourselves whether this was a healthy relationship model or just the one we saw in society and blindly followed.

I had a stable job and provided my family with everything they needed. We had a big apartment and two cars, went abroad on holidays, and invested in education for ourselves and our kids. We had good relationships with our parents and spent many weekends with them.

Everything seemed to be going well, but I could never fully relax and enjoy my life. I couldn't understand why—or perhaps I was too afraid of uncovering the answer and ruining our idyllic image. Anxiety was a constant companion, easing only when I distracted myself with new hobbies. These hobbies became obsessions, consuming all my free time.

From day one, my ex-wife knew about my cross-dressing and tolerated it, though she never encouraged me. I never presented publicly in female clothes, but it became a daily routine at home. To cope, I rationalized my behavior, creating excuses ranging from being raised solely by my mom after my father passed away to being a victim of some global LGBTQ+ propaganda agenda. While these theories fit my reality (with enough mental gymnastics), they were far from the truth.

I had a very limited understanding of transgender people, and conservative stereotypes clouded my perception. I convinced myself that I was just a cross-dresser or fetishist, ignoring the fact that wearing feminine clothing felt natural, rather than arousing. I was ashamed to fully accept myself, so I settled for scraps of self-expression.

We lived like this for six years, believing we were happy because our lives mostly conformed to the traditional family ideal. But we ignored obvious signs to the contrary. Then, our second son was born, and our stable life changed pace and direction. This pregnancy was entirely "hers." She made all the decisions and handled everything. Only she fed the baby and refused to let me help. For some fathers, this would align with traditional gender roles, but not for me. Deep down, I felt betrayed, excluded, and robbed of anticipated joy.

As time passed, we drifted further apart, and my depression grew. I tried to distract myself with new hobbies, which turned into obsessive escapes. But eventually, I grew bored and moved on to something new. The only constant was my gender dysphoria. Back then, I didn't know its name or how to seek treatment.

My first exposure to transgender people came through adult content and media, which shaped my understanding, as it does for many. I developed a strong interest in the topic—not for gratification, but out of admiration. Seeing the physical changes achieved through hormone replacement therapy and gender-affirming surgeries made me feel . . . jealous. I wished to be like them. But I kept these thoughts to myself, afraid of the social stigma.

At the same time, I envied beautiful women. Initially, I thought there might be sexual or romantic interest involved, but I never felt that during my ten-year marriage. The truth was clear: I didn't want to be with them—I wanted to *be* them.

My feelings weren't limited to physical traits. I longed for the mindset, emotions, behavior, and attitudes of a woman. Deep down, I already was a woman; I just hadn't fully realized it yet.

I tried sharing my thoughts with my ex-wife. Knowing her conservative views, I approached the subject cautiously, discussing transitioning cases, LGBTQ+ issues, and homophobia. Her reaction was neutral and indifferent, showing neither understanding nor interest.

Our life might have continued like this for years if not for the war in my country. Eleven months of hiding from missile attacks, preparing to protect my family with a gun, and living without electricity changed me. I avoid discussing this period, but it was crucial for my growth. I stopped fearing change because change became my reality. I don't know how or when my transition would have started without the war, but it undoubtedly accelerated the process and gave me the courage to go all in.

While sitting in the bunker or in the bathroom day after day, I understood more and more that nothing would change in my life on its own, and I should take full responsibility for it. Government, friends, relatives, and spouse didn't want to and couldn't do it for me.

When I, with my ex-wife and kids, managed to get out of the war, we searched for a new place to stay for three months. It was a long journey, but during it, I was convinced that I'd never let fear and anxiety control me. Without those feelings pushing me forward, I wouldn't have been able to find my new home and my new self.

We moved to a country that wasn't very friendly to LGBTQ+ people, but it was the perfect choice for other reasons. Back then, I didn't know I had chosen the city where I'd start my life from zero, where I'd divorce and find new friends and a new partner.

During those times of war and immigration, I didn't have the opportunity to explore my gender identity more, but once we settled, that exploration began with a new, higher intensity. I started searching on social media for other people like me, finding information about the reasons why I felt this way, reading forums, and watching YouTube videos of cross-dressers. At first, I explained it to myself as just an interesting topic, but the further it went, the more I understood I was preparing myself for making it a significant part of my life and maybe someday going "full time."

This phase lasted for a month. Then I came out to my ex-wife as a cross-dresser a couple of days before Christmas. We had a long talk for the whole day during which we discussed how it could be done, how it would impact our life, how I could do it publicly, and what specific steps I should take. My ex-wife listened to me and assured me of her full support. She wasn't surprised by my coming out since she frequently saw me wearing female clothes and showing interest in makeup.

During that talk, I understood that I was making a significant, important step for myself, but something was missing. I didn't pay too much attention to it because of the euphoria filling me from the inside. There was a feeling of relief as tension was released, because there was no need to pretend anymore. I felt a sense of hope for living.

Soon after, I bought makeup and new clothes from the women's section of a department store. I started playing sports and changed my diet to lose weight so I could better fit in my new outfits. I initiated a lot of talks with my ex-wife about traditionally feminine attributes, but mostly she was neutral to it. Sometimes she demonstrated interest, and during those short-lived periods, I believed in her acceptance. For both of us, it was some sort of game without any significant negative consequences. I always kept in mind the thought that I had a chance to go back if something went wrong, so it felt pretty safe for me.

Despite that constant euphoria, there was one issue that still bothered me. All these changes were satisfying my gender-expression needs, but they didn't impact my gender identity. I still had a traditionally male role in the family, I had a male body, and I presented myself to and was perceived by society as a man. This period lasted for two weeks, and I understood I should start searching again.

Thankfully, I found the *Diagnostic and Statistical Manual of Mental Disorders—Fifth Edition* and read about the diagnostics of gender dysphoria. There are six characteristics, two of which should be present for six months for giving a diagnosis of gender dysphoria. I had five out of six. There were no more doubts—I was a transgender woman.

At first, I was afraid and ashamed of it. This idea that I'm a transgender person didn't fit into my image of reality, despite all signs pointing to it. I didn't know how to share this information with my ex-wife, as she was the person whose opinion was the most valuable to me at that time. It was about going from feeling like a woman to becoming and being a woman.

I promised myself that I would never lie to her, even if the truth was harsh and could hurt, and I never broke that promise. I began the talk with her by telling her about other transgender people taking hormone replacement therapy and the changes they had experienced. I didn't know for sure if I'd like to start HRT by myself, so when she asked me about my own plans, I replied, "I don't know."

For several days afterward, I shared with her all the information I found about social and medical transitioning, gender-affirming surgeries, HRT, legal aspects of transitioning, and most importantly, positive stories of other couples where one of the partners transitioned and kept their families together. Those stories were mostly sugar-coated, and they showed only one side of transitioning. They created a false perception of transitioning as a light journey with guaranteed happiness in the end. But they didn't tell about sleepless nights crying, physical and mental pain, and grief for losing your old life and partner. This can be applied to both spouses.

In keeping with the traditional five stages of grief, her first reaction was shock and denial. She was mostly silent. Next came anger, depression, and bargaining. The fifth stage, however, was missing: There was no true acceptance. Back then, I hadn't fully realized it because of the fear, shame, and guilt I felt being a transgender woman.

There were only two options: I transition and we separate, or I transition and we stay together. The question of not transitioning was not on the table, because it was the only possible way for me to stay alive.

During the period of my coming out, my ex-wife spoke words of support and acceptance regarding my identity and the situation. Unfortunately, those words couldn't change the fact that they were the first step leading to our divorce.

The initial stages in my transition were scary: the first permanent body changes, like facial hair removal, talking to a psychiatrist to get a gender dysphoria diagnosis, waiting for blood test results and hoping they would permit me to start HRT, getting a prescription for estradiol, buying it for the first time, applying the first patch, taking the anti-androgen pill—each step was scary because it was all new and unknown. And, like with everything scary, it would have been much easier to go through it while being supported by the people closest to me. Unfortunately, that acceptance was limited to a set of cliché phrases. In reality, I knew she was also scared. I was alone. That fear was suffocating me, but I had to support my ex-wife instead.

I came out to my kids right after coming out to my ex-wife. My younger son, who was only three, wouldn't understand what I was trying to say. He was the first person to start using my new chosen name and female pronouns. Recently, he told me I was always a woman and didn't believe that I ever had a male body.

With my eight-year-old, I had a conversation where I explained how I would change and why it was a necessity for me. I was very lucky to receive his full support and acceptance. It took him a short time to get used to it, but he tried his best.

Then came my coming outs to my mom, other relatives, and friends. Most of them replied with support and assured me of their acceptance, but time showed that reality was quite different from the words they said. They still had this image of the person they knew, and suddenly, that person disappeared and became someone else. They perceived it as a loss of their loved son, grandchild, and friend; and, most importantly, my ex-wife perceived it as a loss of a husband.

To an extent, I can agree with this and understand why it happened that way. I had changed, and the new me had almost nothing in common with the person I was before transitioning. There were visible changes—my body, clothes, hairstyle, manners, voice, gestures. But there was also another side:

the inner one. The way I felt about myself, how I expressed emotions, how I thought, and what I wished for.

One of the few constants that hadn't changed was my love for my closest people. I felt the same warmth, affection, care, and interest toward them. Because of that, their acceptance was important for me, and I didn't want to lose them by any means. Sometimes I caught myself thinking I could self-sacrifice and stop my transition or make it slower. Luckily, those thoughts always went away pretty quickly. I didn't want to reassume the burden of meeting expectations and playing a role.

One of the most painful issues with my ex-wife was intimacy—not the actual act, but the attitude toward it. It turned out that we both wanted the same thing, but due to different reasons, we couldn't give it to each other. In my case, there were two main reasons. First, because of HRT, my body and hormonal levels had changed in a way that made intimacy the "old" way harder for me. Second, it was difficult to let myself feel my own desires and needs. I didn't want to play the "traditional" role, the fake one for me. I was a woman who had been forced to be a man, and I couldn't tolerate it anymore.

When I first started my transition, I didn't feel severe genital dysphoria. I wasn't fully happy with my body, but I could tolerate it. Because of that, I thought I probably wouldn't need major gender-affirming surgeries. However, a couple of months after starting HRT, when I felt the first effects, I understood that my dissatisfaction was growing, and it was getting harder to accept that I had the "wrong" body. By this time, I had learned about sexual reassignment surgeries and came to the realization that one day I would be a patient of a gender-affirming surgeon.

Keeping my promise to tell my ex-wife the truth, I shared these thoughts with her. It took me two weeks to tell her, bit by bit, because of her intense reaction. I explained to her the necessity of this difficult and risky procedure. She understood it but told me she didn't know whether she would ever accept it. For me, it was much better to hear the harsh truth than to live in denial.

Looking back, I understand that this was the end of our marriage. She couldn't live with a woman, and I couldn't live without being one.

We continued living as a family for four months after I started my transition. I presented myself as a woman full time, with nothing left of my old wardrobe. I changed my voice through multiple training sessions, and I felt and behaved in my true gender. I was learning to be the new version of myself. It became much easier for me to understand my ex-wife—her wishes and desires. I showed more signs of care and affection. We went out together and presented ourselves as a lesbian couple, even though we weren't one. At the same time, I was forcing myself to carry my old "male" family roles. Ultimately there was a big conflict within ourselves as individuals and as a couple.

One day, after a long, hard talk, she told me she wanted to visit her parents. The reason she gave was that she missed them and wanted to take a break, leaving our kids with their grandma for a week. We both knew it was just a façade for the real reason—it was the separation.

Once she left, I felt total emptiness, mixed with grief, but at the same time, contentment. It's a very strange combination that I couldn't compare to anything I had ever experienced before. I knew that our mutual suffering had ended, and we had to learn how to live on our own and move forward.

We both felt grief and swung from shock to aggression, denial, and bargaining. But this time, we reached the stage of acceptance. Of course, it came through multiple days of crying, self-blaming, accusing each other, hoping to come back together, and ignoring each other. This process wasn't linear; it was more like stages replacing each other on a swing, with their intensity slowly reduced.

We had discussed separation and divorce before. We had a deal that the kids would stay with my ex-wife, and I would provide for them financially. I would have the right to meet them at any time and spend as much time as I needed. Major decisions regarding the kids would be made only by mutual agreement. Besides being coparents, we agreed to stay friends, which, in the end, didn't happen.

After some time, my ex-wife came back with the kids because I was going to Turkey for facial feminization surgery. We had bought tickets for all of us before making the decision to separate, so we were flying together but with different goals. For me, it was a major step in my transition, and for them, it was a vacation. After that trip, my ex-wife and I didn't see each other again.

We both had a lot of intense work ahead. She had never worked and had to solve her own financial issues and learn to take responsibility for herself. For my part, I had never done housework or lived on my own, so I had to learn how. As it turned out, we both succeeded, and it took much less time than we expected. There was nothing unmanageable facing us, as we had feared, and we managed to replace each other with our own resources.

For two months after separating, we continued talking on the phone and sharing things that were happening in our lives. There were some doubts about whether we had made the wrong decision by separating, but they faded when we remembered our real past. This communication had become a habit; we had gotten used to each other after ten years together, and it was hard to break it. But it was necessary because we couldn't yet move forward, become fully independent, or build new relationships. Having your old partner talking to you several times a week and impacting your life didn't make it easier to let someone else enter and take their place in your life. And I had met that person.

I met my girlfriend online several months after separating from my ex-wife. For both of us, it was a shot in the dark, with no real hope for success. I had anxiety about meeting a "chaser," or a person exploring their gender identity at my expense. She followed her friends' advice to give it a try, without having her own strong feelings about it.

We chatted for a long time, and then spent countless hours on video calls after work. Our first meeting lasted much longer than we expected. Then there was our first trip together, followed by plans for the future. My girlfriend knew from the first day we met online that I was a transgender woman, and it made a big, crucial difference in building our new relationship. Everything was clear and transparent. She knew who I was and the journey I was going through. Several old photos taken before my transition didn't make any difference to her because the person in them was just a stranger she had never seen. It's a strange feeling, telling her about my past life and realizing that life didn't belong to me. The only thing that really matters to us is our present and future.

I feel fully accepted and supported in this new relationship. I'm happy because my partner gives me emotions I could only dream of and hope for. We are a lesbian couple, but this time, a real one.

In conclusion, I would like to say that I'm very grateful for the ten years I spent with my ex-wife and for the two amazing kids we have. I have no regrets about spending this time with her, but we reached a point where staying together meant mutual suffering. For me, it was living without true acceptance and support, forcing myself to follow old family and gender roles. For her, it was living with a completely new and different person to whom she wasn't attracted. Separating was the right decision. Now we're finishing the legal process of divorce, and hopefully, when all the resentment passes, we'll remember the time spent together with a smile and positive emotions.

There is no one to blame for how our situation changed. Transition means changes for both partners, and sometimes we aren't ready to change ourselves and accept that our partners are no longer the same. It's a matter of perspective. For some, that may be understood as a betrayal, but others will see it as the only way to live. We are moving forward.

Acknowledgments

Thank you to: Jamye Waxman, Lev Michael Moses, Ezra Teshome, Rachel Kirkwood, Rhani Remedes, Cooper Lee Bomardier, Autumn Hickman, Sonja Lenz Rashid, Jerry Shapiro, Amanda Kirkhuff, and Mattilda Bernstein Sycamore.

Jacoby Ballard, thank you for all of your support with this book.

Anna Valdez, I am endlessly grateful to have you in my life.

V, together, we have weathered the storms that divorce brought us. I only need to look into your eyes to be assured that I am your father and always will be. I love you!

About the Authors

Paul A. Aguilar is a fourth-generation San Franciscan, with a family history rooted in the city. He witnessed the AIDS epidemic firsthand, losing his first close friend in 1981. After testing positive for HIV in 1988 at the age of twenty-five, Paul became a prominent advocate for people living with HIV/AIDS. He volunteered at AIDS walks and dance-a-thons, sharing his story and promoting the idea of living with HIV rather than dying from it. Paul was involved in implementing Proposition 36, a program that addressed substance abuse as a public health issue. He also worked with immigrants and refugees, and he later joined the San Francisco AIDS Foundation as a long-term survivor community liaison. Paul coauthored "The San Francisco Principles 2020," a manifesto for people living and aging with HIV. He is a resident and board member of Marty's Place, a low-income housing cooperative for people with HIV/AIDS. In 2023, Paul was named Lifetime Achievement Grand Marshal for SF Pride and is currently working on his memoirs.

Jacoby Ballard teaches yoga and Buddhism and resides on Shoshone, Ute, Goshute, and Paiute land in Salt Lake City. He teaches prenatal and postnatal yoga online for queer communities, an extension of his ongoing Queer and Trans Yoga class that is taught both in person and online. Jacoby consults on diversity, equity, inclusion, and justice with yoga and meditation centers and projects, to extend their reach and ground their offerings. He gardens, forages, writes, hikes, sings, and makes art with his child. Learn more at jacobyballard.net.

Thomas Beatie is an author, entrepreneur, and family man.

Dominika Bednarska is a queer disabled femme author from the Bronx who has lived and worked in the East Bay for the last twenty years. Dominika was a Lambda Literary Fellow and a Holloway Postdoctoral Fellow at UC Berkeley, where she completed her PhD in English and disability studies. Her full-length solo show, *My Body Love Story*, appeared at the National Queer Arts Festival at the Garage Theater in San Francisco. She has also performed at Girl Talk, the Marsh, CounterPULSE, Queer Open Mic, Femme Con, Butch Voices, the Society for Disability Studies Annual Conference, the Knitting Factory in New York City, and the Fringe Festival. Her writing has been nominated for a Pushcart Prize in poetry.

Jálynn T. Castleman is a Black, queer, neurodivergent writer, mom, and professional nerd. A contributing writer for Autostraddle, she navigates the intersections of motherhood, divorce, and healing from her third-story walk-up in Brooklyn, New York. When she's not reading, writing, or parenting, you can find her in the kitchen or working on the same sweater she started knitting over five years ago. She hopes to finish it before her three-year-old goes off to college. Visit her at www.jalynncastleman.com.

Paisley Cornell is a licensed marriage and family therapist known for her work with the LGBTQ+ community, particularly transgender and gender-diverse individuals. She specializes in addressing trauma, anxiety, depression, and issues related to gender identity. Paisley is a transgender woman herself, which brings a unique perspective to her practice as she helps clients navigate their own journeys of self-acceptance and healing. In addition to her clinical work, she has been actively involved as a volunteer for the National Suicide Hotline and the Los Angeles LGBT Center, where she facilitates support groups. Before transitioning into therapy, she worked in the television industry as a producer and editor, but her journey of self-transformation led her to find her calling in mental health.

W. E. Cuthbert took the long way to realizing fundamental things about themselves. Then all those things decided to jump out at once. Since 2021, they've become self-identified as trans masculine, nonbinary, autistic, ADHD, disabled, aro/ace, and polyamorous. This knowledge, and being newly self-aware as a creature of political debate from several directions, sparked an accidental late-blooming career writing about the oddly won freedoms that entails. With bylines at the likes of *Metro*, *The Nation*, *Rooted in Rights*, *QueerAF*, and *Trans+ History Week*, their first aim is always to craft stories that center the humanity in being marginalized. They hope this might cause a shift in thought about people often reduced to supposed "controversies." Meanwhile, they indulge their other, equally accidental occupation of writing queer historical fiction.

Rae-Moses Epstein is a fiction writer and former pop culture journalist who has been published by *The Guardian*. Ze writes short stories centering trans for trans love while pursuing zir master in social work. Currently, ze lives with zir dogson in San Diego, the city that saved zir life.

Teré Fowler-Chapman (he/they) is a Black trans poet, educator, and certified life and recovery coach based in Denver. Raised in the Southwest with deep roots in Louisiana, Teré is pursuing an MFA at Antioch University. Author of *M O O N S H i N E*, their work has been featured by TEDx Tucson, NPR, PBS, and *Huffington Post*. Teré is also a Marsha P. Johnson Fellow and a Rocky Mountain Regional Emmy Award nominee, with over ten years in youth work and performing arts. Learn more at terefc.com.

Shào Fù (he/they) is a queer, transmasculine, neurodivergent Asian artist who grew up in a multicultural family and faced the challenges of coming out in a conservative environment. His journey of navigating divorce, family dynamics, and cultural expectations inspires spaces for others to share their stories, exploring the intersections of culture, queerness, and resilience.

R. M. H. is a librarian, artist, and Baptist deacon. After a long midwestern exile, he is thrilled to have returned to his beloved hometown, New Orleans, where he shares his apartment with a very poorly behaved cat. He has enjoyed the opportunity to reconnect with his mother and is pleased to report that making friends in your forties is not as hard as he had been led to believe. In his free time, he enjoys wandering the city on foot, role-playing games, and communal singing.

Liz Hardwick is a coach, facilitator, and writer who lives and works beside the Wind River mountain range in Wyoming. When they are not on Zoom or in the mountains leading coaching expeditions, they are usually building obstacle courses for their kids and avoiding adult tasks that come along with the excruciating mess of midlife. They are a queer, nonbinary dreamer, in perpetual awe of other rural, queer, and trans rabble-rousers making the world more beautiful. Find out more at onewildlifecoaching.com or on instagram @one.wild.life.coaching.

Tahnie Holcomb (they/them) is a middle-aged, still-trying-to-get-divorced, multiracial, survivor, tired but happy parent who is feeling cuter, more confident, and more clear with every week that passes. People often describe Tahnie as having "peaceful," "chill," or "grounding" energy, while good friends may get close-ups of anxiety as well as carefree fun. As far as paid work goes, you can find Tahnie in roles such as healer, writer, consultant, counselor, coach, and more.

Leonardo Kattari (he/they) received his doctorate in social work from Michigan State University and holds a master of social work from the University of Denver. Their research is specifically centered around transgender and gender-diverse individuals and allies, exploring civic engagement and its potential for effecting transformative community change. He has over a decade of practice experience that spans various domains, including health education, health policy, community mobilization and organizing, and advocacy through the art of storytelling. His work is firmly grounded in the principles of community-driven action and data-informed decision-making by striving to advance health equity through civic engagement and transformative systems change.

Shanna Katz Kattari (they/them), PhD, MEd, is an associate professor at the University of Michigan School of Social Work in the Women's and Gender

Studies Department. Kattari is also the director of the [Sexuality | Relationships | Gender] Research Collective. A white, disabled, chronically ill, AuDHD/neurodivergent, Jewitchy, kinky, polyamorous, queer, fat, nonbinary femme, they are an esteemed researcher, educator, and activist whose work has made significant contributions to social work, sexuality, and disability justice spaces. With a steadfast commitment to social justice and equity, Shanna's research and advocacy efforts have focused on understanding and addressing the unique challenges faced by marginalized communities, particularly within the realms of gender, sexuality, and disability (including neurodiversity). Shanna's impact extends far beyond academia, as they work to bridge the gap between research and real-world change, inspiring others to take action and create a more just and inclusive society for all.

Aleks Liou (they/them) is a queer, nonbinary abolitionist, community organizer, and writer working alongside youth activists to build youth-organizing capacity and intergenerational solidarity in grassroots spaces. They live in the Bay Area with their dog, Ponyo.

Marina Montes de Oca is a first-generation Chicanx raised in East Los Angeles who came out as queer to her all-girl Catholic high school in the nineties. She is an ex-Riotgrrrl, sometimes writer, fashion industry veteran, and small business owner. After having her son in 2014, Marina felt disillusioned by the negative impacts of mass consumer manufacturing, so she left her career as the director of marketing for a major premium denim brand to create a sustainably focused, kid-centered brick-and-mortar retail shop. She has a BA in English and business and currently resides in the suburbs, where she shadow dances in her living room to Peel Sessions on vinyl.

Sassafras Patterdale (formerly Lowrey) is a celebrated author whose queer and leather books (*Kicked Out*, *Roving Pack*, *A Little Queermas Carol*, *Leather Ever After*, and *Lost Boi*) have been honored by awards from the American Library Association, the Lambda Literary Foundation, and the International Leather Association. Sassafras's work regularly appears in leading publications such as

The New York Times, *WIRED*, *Catapult*, and *The Rumpus*. Sassafras has taught queer storytelling workshops at colleges, conferences, bookstores, festivals, and squats from Atlanta to Berlin to New York to Oakland to Amsterdam. The film rights to Sassafras's queer leather novel *Lost Boi* were recently optioned. Learn more at www.SassafrasPatterdale.com.

Nailah Rose is a Black transfemme artist, facilitator, and echo of something ancient yet familiar. Through mediums of creative writing, movement, and ritual, she seeks to open portals to Black queer and trans divinity and reckons with the insatiable urge to just become the earth. She's currently a TapRoots Artist in Residence with the North Carolina Climate Justice Collective.

Kira Ry is a transgender woman originally from Ukraine. Kira began her transition later in life after moving to Romania due to the war. Over the course of her journey, she experienced significant changes in beliefs, values, and identity. Kira is currently pursuing a second degree in psychology to help support and guide other transgender individuals. By sharing her story, Kira aims to offer insight, build empathy, and inspire others who are navigating their own journeys.

Chris E. Vargas is a video maker and transdisciplinary artist. He is the executive director of the Museum of Transgender Hirstory and Art, a critical and conceptual arts and hirstory institution highlighting the contributions of trans art to the cultural and political landscape.

Janis Vogel is a certified leadership and relationship coach who has helped dozens of people heal from toxic relationships and careers. Her clients go on to rebuild life and business with confidence. Janis's coaching is powerful because she has been there. She has been divorced twice and has healed from toxic relationships and childhood trauma by building unshakable self-worth and self-love. Now she helps others do the same. Janis worked for decades in the film industry for directors such as Ben Stiller, Celine Song, and Spike Lee. She has cut numerous short films for directors Silas Howard and Heather Acs. Janis's work as a photographer and writer has been published in publications including *Poetry for Coaching: Transformation Through Verse* and *The Brick Journal.* A queer, Black mother of a fierce six-year-old, she grew up on the bucolic island of Martha's Vineyard, cut her teeth as an artist in New York City for thirteen years, and now lives in the tiny beach town of Leucadia, California.

Syd Yang (they/them) is a mixed-race Taiwanese American queer, trans writer and Buddhist chaplain living on Chumash/Tongva land (Los Angeles) who weaves together magic, prayer, and intention as a spiritual counselor through their practice, Blue Jaguar Healing Arts. They tell stories as a liberation practice, slicing open words to release the restorative nectars held within. Their writing locates its resonance at the intersections of Buddhism, sexuality, and mental health and has been shared in a variety of queer, BIPOC, Asian American and Buddhist literary spaces and publications. Their memoir, *Release: A Bulimia Story* (2019) reimagines what spiritually based recovery for marginalized bodies could look like without shame. Learn more at bluejaguarhealingarts.com.

About North Atlantic Books

North Atlantic Books (NAB) is an independent, nonprofit publisher committed to a bold exploration of the relationships between mind, body, spirit, and nature. Founded in 1974, NAB aims to nurture a holistic view of the arts, sciences, humanities, and healing. To make a donation or to learn more about our books, authors, events, and newsletter, please visit www.northatlanticbooks.com.